D1221924

EFFECTIVE CATALOGS

WILEY SERIES ON HUMAN COMMUNICATION

EFFECTIVE CATALOGS

JOHN D. HAUGHNEY
Techdata Associates

JOHN WILEY & SONS, INC.
New York • London • Sydney • Toronto

Library of Congress Catalog Card Number: 68-28503
SBN 471 36030 9
Printed in the United States of America

PREFACE

Effective Catalogs presents sound procedures for producing one of today's basic marketing tools—the company catalog. Although the fundamental approach to catalogs differs considerably in various markets, such as medical, construction, and electronic, there are many common denominators in their catalog programs. *Effective Catalogs* discusses each of the standard activities required to produce a good working catalog as well as the special considerations needed for a particular market.

The material in this book appears in the standard order of performance, starting with the function of management and finishing with catalog distribution. Chapters 1 through 3 which are concerned primarily with management aspects of the catalog program, include items such as planning, budgeting, and scheduling. Chapters 4 through 7 cover the steps required to produce catalog mechanicals for the printer. The role of the catalog coordinator, copy writer, designer and artist are all thoroughly discussed. Chapters 8 and 9 are concerned with printing and distributing the catalog. Also included are helpful suggestions on keeping up-to-date catalog material in the field. Chapter 10 covers a facet in the catalog program often overlooked; that is, the integration of the catalog into an over-all marketing plan. Chapter 11 discusses briefly the role of computer composition for catalog production, which, though relatively new, is fast becoming a factor in the composing field.

Chapter 12 is a summary of common catalog deficiencies. It may prove interesting to evaluate your existing catalog by using the checklist in this chapter. Typical items are indexing, organization, design, and marketing plan. This checklist gives you the opportunity to evaluate a new catalog before it is printed or distributed. Remember, its importance demands this kind of critical analysis. It is impossible to measure in terms of lost sales dollars the effect a poor catalog will have; however, results of good sales catalogs are offered by the many highly successful firms that depend solely on them for sales orders.

JOHN D. HAUGHNEY

Lexington, Massachusetts
January 1968

CONTENTS

EFFECTIVE CATALOGS

INTRODUCTION

Does a good catalog increase sales? Definitely, although having a good catalog is not enough. The catalog must be suitably integrated into an over-all marketing system to obtain maximum results. This book includes all procedures necessary to prepare the most effective catalog program, from the most critical planning stage through catalog distribution. It presents proved methods of obtaining the main objective—more sales at less cost.

Have you ever thought of your catalog as a company representative? Remember, if properly distributed, it remains a full-time salesman, always in contact with prospective buyers. Like a salesman or company representative, the catalog must be informative, well-presented, and in good taste. In many instances the only contact a buyer may have with your organization or product is your catalog. An ineffective catalog, like a poor salesman, could mean a lost order.

Is your catalog easy to use, particularly by a potential buyer? His time is valuable. The catalog must lead him to his item of interest in the shortest possible time. If more than one product or line is included, the catalog must be sectionalized and have a good indexing system. Make ordering as simple as possible. Never forget that your competitor's catalog may be within easy reach.

Is your catalog up-to-date? The fastest way to lose a sale is to have a buyer discover that he is using an obsolete catalog. The methods of catalog maintenance are strongly influenced by product longevity. This book discusses the desirability of complete catalog reprint versus replacement pages.

Do you know your readers? Again we can employ the analogy of the catalog and the salesman, for as the salesman must know his territory, so the catalog producer must know his intended users. Talk their language—know their needs. Promote user readability by using accepted and familiar trade terms.

These questions are intended to illustrate a few of the important and calculated measures that are necessary to implement an effective catalog program. This book discusses in detail the thoughts expressed in the foregoing paragraphs, as well as all pertinent catalog program procedures.

1

CATALOGS . . . YOUR BEST SELLER

The chapter title in no way denies the value of good, hard personal selling; rather, it strongly emphasizes the importance of a comprehensive, well-designed catalog.

Before delving into the many intricacies of a catalog program, you must first attempt to define your potential user or buyer. The more familiar you are with his requirements, the better prepared you are to obtain maximum results. The one and only axiom in a catalog program is: *"Always anticipate your user."* The user must be given prime consideration; all decisions affecting the catalog program must be made with him in mind. This axiom applies equally to industrial, construction, and domestic markets. There are other important considerations for developing a successful catalog program, but none is as important as the buyer. The buyer has no control over how his catalog needs are met. The seller, on the other hand, can assist the buyer by anticipating his needs and, in so doing, benefits himself.

What user reaction are you soliciting and how easy is it to obtain? The answers to these questions usually describe the purpose of a catalog. In a mail order catalog, for example, the user reaction desired is obviously an order via the mails. This simple answer satisfies the first part of the question, but now consider the second—how easy is it to obtain? This is not so simple to answer; nevertheless, it must also be satisfied. A typical user of a mail order catalog may be a person who knows what he wants and needs only to be directed to the right page to determine prices and model numbers. This person is best served by an effective indexing system. Another user may be interested in a general product area and may want to investigate all related products before making a purchase. This man will appreciate a well-organized catalog in which products are logically grouped. A third typical user may be a browser who wishes to peruse the catalog at his own pace; interesting presentations will attract his attention. For all three of the typical users described there is one common item for you to consider—the order form. The form must be made as simple as possible. This facilitates ordering by the buyer and order handling within your plant.

Not all catalogs are designed to sell directly. This is especially true in the industrial market in which a sales call or some personal contact between the seller and buyer is usually essential to resolve details and extract an order. The primary objectives of an industrial market catalog are to create product interest and to influence potential buyers to invite your representatives to call.

Catalogs prepared for the construction market also are not usually designed to sell directly. In the construction market the specifying architect and engineer are the key factors. Although it is necessary to sell the general contractor, builder, and owner, the primary buying influences in building construction are the architects and their engineers. Strong recommendations by them usually mean a sale for you. The buying influence of architects and engineers is exerted through drawings and specifications that determine how a building is to be constructed or modified, what materials are to be used, and how the building is to be equipped. Catalogs for the construction market must give the architect and engineer all the information needed to select intelligently the right product for the right job. Guide form specifications should be included in the catalog to assist them in preparing a product specification to be included with the over-all building specification (details on guide form specification writing are given later in this book). A product specified is not necessarily a product sold. An effective follow-up system must be employed to ensure that the architect and engineer are not persuaded later to use another product. The catalog remains in the center of the sales action until the specification is written. Follow-up action must be initiated by your salesmen or distributors.

In all the examples the focal point is the user. Whether you want him to order directly from the catalog, to invite your sales representatives to call, or to specify your product, the ultimate objective is increased sales at a lower cost. *"Always anticipate your user."*

CATALOGS ARE FULL-TIME SALESMEN

Most facets of a catalog are analogous to the attributes of a salesman. There is one major advantage, however, that a salesman has over a catalog, and that is personal contact. The good salesman has an opportunity to feel his way along during a sales interview, or, in other words, "play it by ear." In many cases this opportunity can be decisive. A catalog will never be given this chance. It is always very important, therefore, to give the best available catalog treatment to your products; the catalog may be given only one chance.

Both catalog and salesman must be informative, attractive, and well-presented. Many good products fail to get proper consideration because of poor promotion by either a salesman or catalog. The salesman during his personal contact should have the knowledge to answer intelligently questions concerning a product. Conversely, the catalog must anticipate all inquiries, and substantial related material must be included to satisfy the potential client's needs.

Do not underestimate the importance of the physical appearance of a catalog or salesman. Smart appearance instills confidence and reflects dignity, stability, and authoritativeness. These qualities will always enhance your sales efforts. An unkempt appearance suggests uncertainty and lack of confidence. The first impression is the most important; make it a good one!

Good presentation, although mentioned last, is as important as an informative and attractive catalog. A logical presentation makes the catalog easy to use. Presentation means a great deal more than a good layout. It embraces both content and format, which include the type and amount of information to be given. A potential client must be given the shortest path to his item of interest; his time is important. Related items should be grouped together. A poorly organized catalog will be used once, at best, and then only by persons with enough leisure time to solve your puzzle.

What are the advantages that a catalog has over the salesman? Foremost is its persistence. Once distributed, it remains as your steadfast salesman, always in contact with prospective buyers. A catalog in the field must be supported by an advertising program; otherwise it will be buried in the dust of a bookshelf or desk drawer. In industrial and construction markets advertising in trade magazines and journals is the most effective method of supporting your catalog and promoting your company's sales efforts. Whenever practical, mention the catalog in your advertisements.

Another important asset of a catalog program is the economical means it provides to introduce a product to all potential customers. The cost of mailing a catalog is negligible when compared with the cost of a sales call. Many catalogs could be mailed around the world for the price of one call by a salesman.

A catalog can be used to train new salesmen or, when there is large product diversification, as a handy reference book by veteran salesmen.

The combination of a good catalog, a follow-up advertising program, and a salesman is invaluable in projecting the image of your company and in promoting its products and, ultimately, its continuous growth.

TYPES OF CATALOG

The most basic catalog is the general catalog, which usually contains the complete product line of a company or, in the case of larger companies, the product line of each division. The question often arises: "What should we include in the catalog"? The best way to answer this is with another question. "If the product is worth manufacturing, is it not worthy of cataloging?" Every attempt should be made to give equal treatment in the catalog to all manufactured products. If an investment is made to produce an item, the product should be adequately supported in the company catalog program. In many instances only the popular items are given complete treatment in the catalog, whereas slow-moving items get, at best, a brief mention. This single fact may be the reason why the slow-moving items are not selling. An unequal catalog presentation suggests to a potential user that those items not emphasized in the catalog are secondary lines in your business. An immediate reaction of a potential client might be to select a competitor's catalog that gives full treatment to his item of interest.

Another risk in using incomplete data in a catalog is improper product ordering by the client. A great source of disillusionment is receiving something other than what you have ordered. The ill will created is never forgotten. Every effort should be made to facilitate ordering and eliminate aggravation.

A second type of catalog is the product line or, special catalog. In many cases this catalog will duplicate information contained in the general catalog. A product line catalog may not be necessary. Ideal applications include coverage for seasonal products, special sale announcements, or companies with a wide variation of product lines. The foremost advantage of product line catalogs is that they are smaller than the general catalog. Catalog size in most instances influences catalog usability. An "easy-to-use" catalog is soon recognized and quickly becomes habit-forming. The major goal for all catalogs is to become the "Bible" of the industry, for with such recognition, the battle is half won.

CATALOG LANGUAGE

When determining catalog language, we must again consider the user. Look at your catalog from the viewpoint of your potential customers. Are you communicating properly by speaking his language? How difficult is it for an individual to take the necessary steps in buying your product? Beginning with the instant he recognizes the need for the type of product you make, what information does he desire? Obviously, catalog presentation for industrial markets will differ drastically from presentations for domestic markets, but only because of the reader. A transistor catalog would emphasize technical information on transistor characteristics for the electrical design engineer, whereas a presentation in a furniture catalog would be slanted toward the esthetic appeal for the average individual; for example, in cataloging home furnishings you would place them in distinctive settings. Many readers will project themselves into these settings that compliment your products. This initial interest is created not by the size or color of a piece but by the elegance of the over-all picture. Furniture dealers go to great lengths to present their lines in elaborate and consumer-oriented showrooms to create the initial impression that may ultimately be the determining factor of the sale. Catalog designs for this market should follow this reasoning.

SUMMARY

In order for a catalog to be most effective the right information must be given to the right people at the right time. A catalog must be supported by an effective follow-up system. You must examine your catalog from the viewpoint of your potential user to see how it rates as a product information service. To encourage increased sales your service to buyers should start before they buy from you. Your catalog should be distributed to all potential clients in your area of interest.

Your catalog represents your biggest showroom and most persistent sales force. Logically, it should be the best you can offer. When is the last time you have taken a long, hard look at your present catalog? Do you take it for granted or consider it a necessary evil? If you do, just imagine how your potential consumers regard it. The following chapters describe all phases of a catalog program from the beginning (planning) to the end (distribution and follow-up).

2

PLANNING YOUR CATALOG

There is no standard pattern for producing a sales catalog; however, certain basic criteria are essential to the development of all successful catalog programs. Each program must be carefully analyzed so that the best possible results can be achieved. Good management, so vital to any progressive organization, is most important when developing an effective catalog. The key to good management is thorough planning. Planning could start with a "kick-off" meeting for all those concerned with the basic purpose of establishing a program milestone chart.

A catalog coordinator should be assigned immediately. He should have thorough knowledge of all the mechanics of a catalog program and he should be given the authority and principal responsibility for the production of the catalog from inception to completion. His first task is to organize a field research survey. Good catalog planning begins with such a survey. At this early stage the experience of potential clients can be helpful. Sales representatives and distributors have undoubtedly received many comments about an old catalog or a competitor's sales catalog; call on them and obtain their views. All opinions, suggestions, and observations, whether critical or favorable, should help guide you in the right direction. The basic objectives are to retain the best features of the old catalog and correct any obvious weaknesses.

How is this information solicited? Mailed questionnaires and personal interviews are the most efficient methods. A sample of a typical questionnaire is given in Figure 1, but do not feel limited by the items listed. Additional items related to a particular market should be added. Do not, however, infringe on too much of a potential user's time. Personal interviews can be made by using the items listed in the questionnaire.

After compiling a significant number of completed questionnaires and interview sheets, a thorough analysis of the information is made. In order to apply sound procedures to improve your catalog, interpret all pertinent

7

QUESTIONNAIRE FOR NEW CATALOG

1. *Catalog Size*—Please indicate preference.

    a. Retain present (8½ × 11) format _____
    b. Change to smaller size format _____
    c. State reason for preference _____
    _____
    _____

    d. If smaller, what size do you recommend? _____

2. *Catalog Binding*—Please indicate preference.

    a. Retain present sewn binding _____
    b. Change to loose leaf ring binder _____
    c. Change to spiral metal binder _____
    d. Change to plastic binding _____
    e. State reason for preference _____
    _____
    _____

3. *Catalog Cover*—Please indicate preference.

    a. Retain present hard paper cover _____
    b. Change to soft, flexible paper cover _____
    c. Change to flexible plastic cover _____
    d. Change to stiff plastic cover _____
    e. State reason for preference _____
    _____
    _____

4. *Color*—Please indicate preference.

    a. Use single color inside _____
    b. Use second color inside _____
    c. Other comments on color _____
    _____
    _____

5. *Type Size*

    a. Type size used in existing catalog is satisfactory _____
    b. Favor changing to larger size type _____
    c. Favor changing to smaller size type _____
    d. Other comments on type size _____
    _____
    _____

6. *Type Face*

    a. Type face used in existing catalog is satisfactory _____
    b. Favor using another type face _____
    c. Specify by name or by reference to another publication any type face you
    would recommend.
    _____

d. Other comments on type face _____

_____

7. *Illustrations*

   a. Pictures and line drawings in existing catalog are satisfactory: Yes _____
      No _____
   b. Recommend that pictures and line drawings be made:
      Larger _____ Smaller _____
   c. Other comments

   _____

   d. Would you favor use of a color background or panel to set off illustrations?
      Yes _____ No _____

   e. Other comments on color _____

   _____

8. *Indexing*

   a. Is some form of page indexing desirable?
      Yes _____ No _____
   b. If yes, do you favor tab, trimmed, or notched index pages? _____
   c. Other comments on indexing _____

   _____

9. *Organization*

   What suggestions can you offer about the organization or order of presentation?

   _____

   _____

10. *Layout*

    Based on the existing catalog, do you have any suggestions or criticisms about
    the layout of material on individual pages?

    _____

    _____

11. *Tables of Dimensions*

    What changes, if any, would you recommend in the tables of dimensions as
    they appear in the present catalog?
    a. For example, could the tables be simplified or made more compact in any
       way?

    _____

    _____

Figure 1. Typical catalog survey questionnaire.

facts to obtain a better understanding of precisely what data potential catalog users need. This understanding is necessary to arrive at decisions and to judge the relative merits of these decisions in relation to their effect on production time, cost, and acceptable standards for the catalog. Pay particular attention to troublesome and weak areas. Develop these areas. The results of this effort will make the catalog easier to use. Transforming a mass of technical data into a meaningful, organized catalog is an immense challenge. Discriminating between essential and nonessential information from the user's viewpoint is the first important step.

USING AN AGENCY

Before continuing the discussion of catalog planning, the subject of using an agency for catalog preparation is explored. Are the talents necessary to produce a catalog available within your company? In many instances they are not, thus making it almost imperative to seek out an agency. There are many advantages to employing a competent agency. Agencies specialize in the creation and preparation of all types of sales literature; they are continuously searching for new and imaginative methods of promoting products and services; their business is knowing how to motivate people by sales literature; and their staffs are concerned daily with the mechanics of economically organizing, compiling, and producing effective catalogs. These statements are not intended to suggest that an agency should be selected, turned loose, and left alone. Close coordination between the manufacturer and agency is essential.

How should an agency be selected? The prime consideration is the product. If it is for the domestic market, most advertising agencies should be suitable. In the industrial and construction markets look for agencies with technical competence. An agency with this capability is prepared to communicate with potential buyers in industrial and construction markets which are usually more technical than the domestic market. Ask to see samples of agency-prepared catalogs in related areas. Most agencies, at no obligation, will analyze products, markets, and a catalog program and submit a proposal based on their evaluation. An agency's proposal is the most concrete evidence on which to base a selection. Study all proposals and compare them to the catalog program specifications. Use any submitted recommendation that will improve the proposed program. If the choice of an agency is not apparent after reviewing all proposals, price may be used as the decisive factor. Although price is always a significant factor, it should not be the only element considered during selection. Poorly prepared and designed catalogs, no matter what they cost, are expensive when considering sales opportunities lost. The proposal containing the most comprehensive program of good catalog design, format, presentation, quality production, and advertisement coordination should be given every consideration.

CATALOG SPECIFICATIONS

The next step in catalog planning is preparing detailed catalog specifications to be approved by all the company departments concerned. To prepare these detail specifications, the coordinator must draw upon his knowledge of catalog mechanics and apply it to the results of the field survey. The catalog specification should include statements on the following items:

1. Catalog objectives
2. Description of potential buyer
3. List of products to be cataloged
4. Product technical data
5. Catalog theme
6. Catalog outline
7. Number of illustrations (photographs and line art)
8. Type of presentation preferred (test, tabular, graphical)
9. Type of composition (selection of type face)
10. Number of colors to be used
11. Selection of paper stock
12. Binding
13. Suggestions for cover designs and cover material
14. Quantity of catalogs to be printed (types of printing processes)
15. Method of distribution
16. Advertisement support

1. *Catalog objectives.* Having a statement of catalog objectives is important not only during the planning phase of the catalog but also during the preparation. Many decisions must be made during the generation of a catalog. Before making decisions it is helpful to review the catalog objectives to determine what answers are most likely to achieve desired results.

The basic objective is to produce a catalog that will be most useful to the users or buyers for whom it is intended and thereby increase sales probabilities. The catalog objective should also contain a statement on the desired user reaction—an order direct from the catalog, an invitation for a sales representative to call, or a specified product. Add any statements related to products that substantiate the existence of a catalog.

2. *Description of potential buyer.* Before attempting to describe potential buyers or users, make a list of titles or descriptive names of the persons most likely to be interested in your products. Knowing who they are will aid in the preparation of distribution lists; knowing what they are helps to define a class of people and their needs. Review the list carefully and look for common factors that will suggest the tone and slant of the catalog presentations. Remember, this group is the only reason for preparing a catalog; the more that is known about them, the better prepared you are to motivate them to buy.

3. *List of products to be cataloged.* A detailed list of products should be compiled and included in the catalog specifications. This list is important because it determines the size or page count and space allotment of the proposed catalog. During the preparation phase it is a reference list for collecting data and planning photography.

4. *Product technical data.* To determine what product technical data should be included review the catalog objective, the description of the buyer, and the list of products. Include the data most likely to be needed by the prospective buyer so that the catalog will do the job for which it was intended. Typical technical data includes dimensions, weights, types of finish, colors, mounting information, electrical characteristics, tolerances, and so forth.

5. *Catalog theme.* The catalog should have a central theme to help promote enthusiastic response, to knit the catalog together, and to make the data flow more easily. For products that are more technical a theme is not always possible. If this is the case, try to develop a family resemblance in the technical presentation. Using a second color is the simplest method of establishing a standard presentation format.

6. *Catalog outline.* A catalog, like any other publication, should not be started before an outline is prepared. The outline reflects the organization of the catalog; it is a map or battle plan; and it helps to prevent straying from the main purpose of the catalog. Include as many details as possible. The list of products to be cataloged, the products to be photographed, and the proposed method of indexing should be included. The outline is the basic tool for planning, for determining an accurate page count, for appropriating space, for preparing a budget, and for following production progress once the program is begun.

7. *Number of illustrations (photographs and line art).* The most concrete evidence one can offer a potential buyer, without his actually seeing the product, is a photograph. The often-quoted phrase "a picture is worth

10,000 words" certainly applies if the picture is in a catalog. A line drawing or rendering is a poor substitute for a photograph. In many cases illustrations are the most important part of a catalog, and a photographic illustration portrays a product accurately. Poor illustrations are subject to confusion and are frequently the cause of incorrect ordering or specifying. The use of photographic illustrations is recommended. Try to make photographs interesting and pay particular attention to subject lighting in order to reduce retouching costs.

What type of photographs should be used? Again, we must look at the potential reader. For the domestic market attractive settings and colorful human interest shots are most effective. For the industrial market individual product shots are usually all that is required. A combination of individual product shots and typical installation photographs are used to best advantage for the construction market.

Often the terms photograph and "halftone" are interchanged. Technically this is incorrect. A photograph is a print processed from the camera negative of the original shooting. A halftone is best described as a printer's process used to produce printed reproductions of a photograph in a publication (refer to Chapter 8 for additional details).

Normally, line art lacks the reader impact that a photograph has; however, there are many areas in which line art can be used beneficially. The most common applications of line art in catalogs are dimensional outline drawings, cross-sectional views, and wiring diagrams.

8. *Type of presentation.* Most common presentations include text and tabular, graphical, and pictorial material. Use the presentation that will be most useful to a reader. Keep arrangements simple. Avoid using unusual patterns; save them for advertisements. The eye is accustomed to symmetrical layouts.

9. *Type of composition.* The two methods of composition used in catalog preparation are cold-type and hot-metal composition. Generally, hot metal is more popular because it offers greater flexibility. Cold-type composition is usually more economical.

Cold-type composition is produced by IBM, VariTyper, Justowriter and equivalent typewriter-like machines. The machines should be electrically operated, proportional-spaced, with pressure control to provide constant key strike. It is important to use carbon ribbon and high quality paper to assure that each character will be the same weight and density. A proportional-spaced machine has an added capability over a regular typewriter; it can justify both left- and right-hand margins. A regular typewriter uses one space for each character regardless of the character's size. The proportional-spaced machine uses spaces in proportion to the width of the character. For example, the letter "w" is much wider than the letter "l" and, therefore, uses more space. To justify both left- and right-hand margins copy must be typed twice. The first typing is needed to determine character count and proper spacing; the second typing produces the justified copy. Special training is required for proportional-spaced machine operators.

The IBM and Justowriter machines are similar. Both are built somewhat like a standard electric typewriter and the most common type faces used on them are No. 1 Bold and Modern. These faces are shown in Figure 2. There are some machines available with italic and sans serif faces. The main disadvantage of these machines is that the operator cannot change type size, weights, or face.

The Justowriter, unlike the IBM machine, can be operated by a punched

called "composition" and can be used for either letterpress or offset reproduction. However your typewriter could do a better job if it had all

ABCDEFGHIJKLMNOPQRSTUVWXYZ
abcdefghijklmnopqrstuvwxyz1234567890[‡#$%¢:,]

(a)

type, originally intended for letter use. The fit is loose (it sets at the same escapement as Bold-face #1, although it is 2 points smaller), and the "feel" is informal.

ABCDEFGHIJKLMNOPQRSTUVWXYZ
abcdefghijklmnopqrstuvwxyz 1234567890

(b)

Figure 2.   Common type faces. (a) IBM No. 1 Bold. (b) IBM Modern.

tape or an operator. Once the punched tape is started through the machine, it controls the entire typing process. Several initial conditions must be established before the tape is started and, of course, a first typing by an operator is required to punch the tape. The major advantage of a Justowriter over the IBM is that it justifies right-hand margins automatically. Counting of characters and second typing by an operator are not required.

Type faces can be changed at any time during the typing of copy on VariTyper machines. By tastefully mixing type faces a more interesting and functional presentation can result. To change type faces the machine operator simply replaces fonts. This reduces the production rate somewhat, but in most cases the results are worth the additional production costs. The flexibility of the machine is determined by the number of available fonts.

Cold-type composition is best used in sales literature such as price lists and form letters. It is not recommended for sales catalogs, mainly because it restricts versatility in design. A recent development in computerized cold-type composition may change the picture drastically. This is discussed briefly in Chapter 11.

There are thousands of hot-metal type faces available to the catalog designer today. Because of the number of faces and the importance of proper type selection to over-all catalog presentation, an entire chapter is devoted to this subject (Chapter 6).

10. *Number of colors to be used.* In the printing industry the number of colors refers to the number of inks used. A one-color job means one ink—normally, but not necessarily, black. At least one additional color should be used in catalogs. This helps add distinction and eye appeal to the catalog. Even more important, a second color can be used to separate individual elements on a page, to add emphasis, to break up large areas of type, to help tie two-page spreads together, and to provide a more effective method of indexing. Adding colors adds cost—costs to print and to prepare copy. The importance of the catalog, however, supports the use of at least one additional color.

When additional colors are used separate printing plates must be prepared for each color. If the color elements of a page do not meet or overlap, all material for that page can be pasted up on the same surface. The printer must be supplied a color key or guide with the pasted-up material that clearly defines the intended color scheme of the final, printed piece.

If the color elements of a page meet or overlap, some form of color separation is required. The most common method used is the building

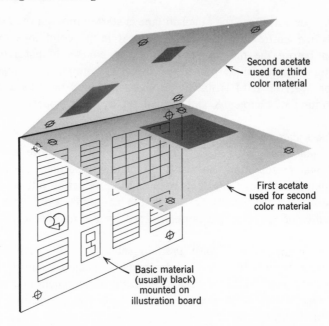

Second acetate
used for third
color material

First acetate
used for second
color material

Basic material
(usually black)
mounted on
illustration board

Figure 3.   Building a typical page mechanical.

of page mechanicals. This method is illustrated in Figure 3. First, the
basic copy or material (usually all black elements) is pasted up on illustration board. Second, the elements of the second color are pasted up
on an acetate or vellum overlay which is hinged to the basic illustration
board. Another overlay must be added for each additional color. All over-
lays should be made to the same scale as the basic board and have correctly placed register marks. Careful preparation of page mechanicals will
always result in a more economical printing bill.

Another form of color separation is called process color. The color
separation is done by the camera and by appropriate filters from copy
prepared in full color. Separate copy exposures are made through red,
green, and blue screened filters. Each filter passes only part of the total
light transmitted from the copy. The negative developed from each of
the exposures is used to prepare the color plates. Usually a fourth exposure
(black) is made to help produce greater density or sharpness than is
possible with only the three basic colors. Additional exposures with special
filters can be used for a particularly demanding job.

Note that the term "screened filters" is used above. A screened filter
is used to break up the copy into tiny dots, which, when reproduced,

are blended easily in the reader's eye to recreate the original copy. The screened or dotted pattern of each color filter is minutely offset from the dot pattern of the other colors so that overprinting, which would result in low quality coloration fidelity, does not occur. The printer should always provide progressive proofs for color checks and for close representation of the final printed material. Additional information on the preparation of mechanicals is given in Chapter 7.

11. *Selection of paper stock.* The selection of paper stock should be coordinated with a printer and, if possible, with the paper manufacturers. Fine appearance or low price means little if the paper will not perform properly and consistently for the printer. In all probability the printer will save money by running better grade, high performance paper rather than a less expensive paper that does not perform consistently and produces large running waste. Usually paper spoilage in the printing operation runs from 3 to 10 percent, depending on the press run.

The major consideration in paper selection is the method of printing (a discussion of printing is given in Chapter 8). Offset lithography is the most popular printing process used for the production of sales catalogs, although letterpress printing is still employed. Both printing methods can be performed on sheet-fed or web presses. The choice of presses is determined exclusively by the quantity of printed catalogs needed. Since press set-up time is considerably longer and more costly for web presses than for sheet-fed presses, runs of more than 50,000 copies are needed to justify the use of the web press. Continuous improvements and modifications in the web-press field could lower this figure in the not-too-distant future.

No matter what printing method or press the printer uses he is interested in the following characteristics of paper stock; mechanical and dimensional stability, drying quality, printing and ink holdout factors, surface bond, folding properties, and consistency. These characteristics are mentioned only to acquaint the reader with some of the printer's problems so that he may be more sympathetic to the printer's recommendations for paper stock.

The appearance properties of paper stock in brightness, opacity, gloss, bulk, and tint are also important. Appearance begins with stock brightness, which is related directly to the type and brightness of the pulp. Pigments, including clays, titanium dioxide, calcium carbonate, and dyes, are used to help improve over-all brightness. Groundwood contributes to paper opacity but unless it is bleached it will generally reduce brightness. Clays are often used to increase opacity, but for high opacity papers titanium or zinc pigments are added. Smooth gloss finishes require a special coating, which is flowed onto the surface of the paper with adhesive additives and then supercalendered, or finished, with very smooth paper rollers. All catalog material should be printed on coated paper. Coated paper adds a distinctive, rich, quality appearance. Some coated paper is made with dull finish clays that are not calendered as much as high gloss paper. This is the basic difference between dull-coated and gloss-coated papers. The dull-coated paper is used best in catalog material that includes heavy text, graphs, and charts that require extensive reading and evaluating by the user.

Bulk, thickness, weight, and caliper are terms that are used to describe paper. Technically it is incorrect to interchange these terms; however, there is no need to define each in this text. To avoid confusion, simply ask your printer to make up a dummy catalog with the estimated number of pages for the new catalog. This will give the exact size, bulk, and weight of the new catalog. This is an important item at this planning stage because mailing and distribution costs can now be determined on a firm basis.

Tinted paper stock is another way of adding distinctive appearance to a catalog. If it is used, the color should be selected carefully. No heavy, bright, offensive colors should be used in a general catalog. Tinted paper stock shortens the life of the catalog and is used best in brochures and advertising pieces. Using different colored paper for various sections in the catalog provides an effective indexing method. This is not always possible and depends on the printing and binding methods used.

12. *Binding.* Generally the binding process consists of gathering pages in proper sequence and combining them under a single cover. There are four popular catalog binding processes: (a) case, (b) perfect or softcover, (c) saddlewire, and (d) mechanical binding. Each is shown in Figure 4.

Case binding is the most conventional method of binding used in bookmaking. A typical case-bound book has sewed, printed signatures pasted by means of endpapers to a rigid cover. A self-aligning process also can be used. In this method the first page of the first signature and the last page of the last signature take the place of endpapers to paste the sewed signatures to the cover. A signature is a term that describes the printer's page layout when more than one page is printed at a time. Printing by signatures provides many printing savings, especially on large press runs. The pages of a signature must conform to a pattern compatible with the printer's automatic folding machinery. The page pattern used in a signature is called imposition. Signatures are made up of 4-, 8-, 12-, 16-, 24-, 32-, 48-, 96-, and 128-page forms. The size of the signature depends on the available press. When printing larger signatures, the paper thickness

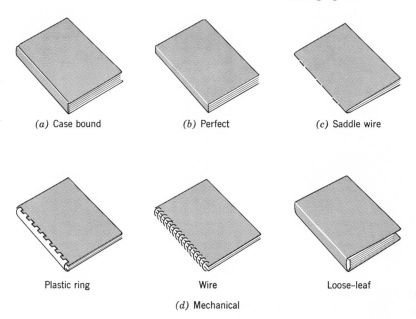

| (a) Case bound | (b) Perfect | (c) Saddle wire |

| Plastic ring | Wire | Loose-leaf |

(d) Mechanical

Figure 4.   Types of catalog Bindings.

becomes a factor. Heavy papers crease, buckle, and have a tendency to spring open. Signatures are discussed in more detail in Chapter 8.

Case binding, although the most conventional binding process used today, is not often suitable for catalog binding except when large runs (more than 50,000) make it economical.

Perfect binding is similar to the process of producing paper pads. The signatures of the catalog are sewed and the back folds are trimmed off. The trimmed side is usually roughened to provide a larger paper surface for more effective gluing. Before the gluing process, however, the signatures are squeezed firmly in a heavy press so that the finished product will be compact. Glue is then applied to the trimmed side (spine) and the outside cover is applied. Catalog thickness should exceed ⅜-inch before considering perfect binding. The perfect-binding process is not recommended for books or catalogs printed on highly coated, heavy paper stocks, for the binding will not hold up with normal use. In such cases catalogs must be designed to withstand abuse.

Saddle stitching is the most economical method of holding catalog pages and cover together. Both the cover and catalog pages are processed so that the product before stitching is a series of folded two-page spreads.

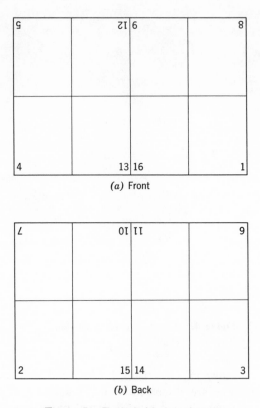

(a) Front

(b) Back

Figure 5.   Typical 16-page signature.

The binding is accomplished by passing two or three staples through the fold in the cover and pages. Paper thickness and the number cf pages are limiting factors in saddle stitching. The tension placed on the center spread increases as the page count increases. Too much tension will cause the center spread to tear and fall out and a large catalog will not close flat. If saddle stitching is planned for a catalog exceeding 100 pages, have a catalog dummy made with the proposed paper stock to ensure that the end product is satisfactory.

Mechanical binding is available in many variations. The term means that some metal or plastic mechanical device, such as screw posts, rings, or wire, secures the pages and cover. Although these devices vary considerably, the binding method differs only in the way that each is attached. As in all binding operations, the signatures or sheets are first collated, but for the mechanical binding all four sides are trimmed. Next, the holes needed for the mechanical binding devices are punched and, last, the devices are applied. There is almost no limit to catalog size (number of pages) for mechanical binding, and it probably is the most popular binding method, especially for smaller catalog press runs.

Another factor to be considered before deciding on the binding is catalog maintenance or up-dating. Product improvements and changes demanded by today's consumer make catalog up-dating a continuous problem. Often this problem is best solved by reissuing a revised catalog. In other cases it might be easier to prepare new or revised pages and distribute them. If this is the case, a binder must be selected so that new or revised pages can be inserted. There are many factors to be considered before selecting a method. The most significant argument against loose-leaf catalogs is that few people will take the trouble to insert the new material sent to them. A loose-leaf catalog is the most economical way to handle changes; there are savings in production, printing, and mailing costs. It should be easy to revise catalogs for industrial and construction markets, but the contents of catalogs for basic consumer markets change so frequently that they are usually reissued.

13. *Suggestions for cover designs and cover material.* It may seem premature to think about cover designs and material at this stage of catalog preparation, but the costs involved are significant. There are three basic methods of applying information to a cover: (a) printing, (b) silk-screening, and (c) stamping.

On a printed cover almost any design can be used within the printable characteristics of the cover material. The most popular cover materials include paper cover stock, various plastic coated materials, and cloth. (Cloth is used on case-bound catalogs.) Paper cover stock can be specified in point (8 point, 10 point, and so forth) or in pounds (70 lb., 80 lb., and so forth). To avoid confusion, ask a supplier for samples before specifying. Paper cover stock gives the printer the fewest problems, especially if the catalog has an elaborately designed cover.

A typical paper cover stock is made of kraft paper, resin impregnated with a coating of lacquer or pyroxylin. After printing, additional durability can be obtained by adding a thin coating of plastic or cellulose.

The plastic materials available are mainly vinyls with paper backings. Vinyl covers offer rigidity, but a critical balance between heat-resistant and cold-resistant capabilities must be maintained. The heat-resistant characteristics affect material stretching and sticking. Without the proper cold-resistant properties the vinyl with cold-crack when exposed to low temperatures. Ink repulsion can also cause problems for the printer.

For case-bound catalogs a specially prepared white cloth stock is available which is suitable for offset printing. This stock is popular for text and reference books. The cloth can be plastic impregnated (pyroxylin or vinyl) and so adds a water repellant feature. Cloth manufacturers stock many colors in several grades. Obtain a swatch book from a printer or cloth manufacturer. Discuss the catalog application with him and evaluate his recommendations before making a decision.

Originally silk-screen printing was a handcraft. A fine mesh screen is prepared with all nonprinting areas blocked out. The screen is then stretched taut over the cover material and ink is applied or squeezed through the open, fine mesh. More recently, machinery has been developed that increases the production rate. Silk screening, however, is more expensive, especially for long runs. The advantages of silk screening are (a) it can be used on any kind of cover material (including coarse cloth) and (b) it may be completely opaque paint that can be applied in layers to simulate embossing. The inks used may have metallic or flat finishes and may be applied very thinly or heavily enough to cast a shadow.

There are many silk-screen suppliers but few with machinery for long-run catalog work. Do not let this be an inhibiting factor if the cover design, material, and production run are suitable. Check these points with a printer and obtain prices from several suppliers.

Stamping is a very popular process used in the production of catalog covers. There are two basic types of stamping—cold and hot. Cold stamping is quite similar to letterpress printing. The main difference is that the die pressure for cold stamping is heavier. The increased die pressure drives the raised area into the cover material to place the ink below the surface. This adds durability to the cover printing and prevents the ink from being rubbed off easily. After the leaf is applied each cover is brushed lightly with fine steel wool to remove excess leaf.

The hot-stamping process is used to apply leaf, for blank or blind impressions, or by embossing. Heat is required to transfer the leaf from its carrier or to help mold the cover material for blind stamping and embossing.

Leaf rolls are available in a variety of colors (metallic or flat). As shown in Figure 6, the leaf is placed between the die or stamp and the cover material. When the hot die is pressed into the cover material the pigments from the leaf are transferred into the weave or grain of the cover material. It is possible to apply several different color leafs during one die impression.

Blank or blind stamping is accomplished by the above process but without leaf. The die heat causes a change in the color and texture of the cover material, leaving a distinct impression. When case-bound covers

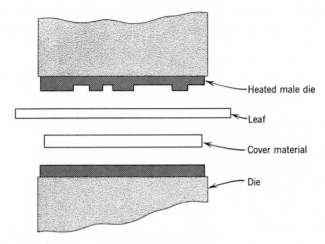

Figure 6. Hot stamping with leaf.

are used the blank or blind stamping should be imposed on the board as well as the cloth material for a more indelible impression. Embossing produces raised impressions. Usually this requires male (convex) and female (concave) dies, as shown in Figure 7. The female die is stamped on top of the cover material with the matching male die positioned under the material. If the impression is simple, the female die may be all that is necessary.

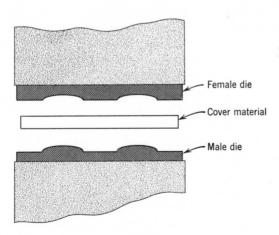

Figure 7. Embossing.

The process used to place the cover design on the cover must be compatible with the design used. Consult a printer for recommendations.

14. *Quantity of catalogs to be printed.* The quantity of catalogs produced decides the method of printing and is a very significant cost factor. The different methods of printing are discussed in Chapter 8. The basic printing alternatives are sheet-fed presses and web-fed presses. At present, runs of fewer than 50,000 are usually considered uneconomical for web presses. Ten years ago this figure was 80,000 to 100,000. Vast improvements have been made and are being made in web-fed presses. It is advisable to obtain prices for both methods if a catalog run is near the dividing point of 50,000 copies.

There are no magic formulas, only common sense, for determining the number of catalogs to print. If there are 20,000 potential clients, print at least 20,000 catalogs. If only 10,000 copies are printed, how can it be determined which half of the potential market will receive catalogs? They may be sent to the wrong half. Good business sense is not based on luck. The cost of producing the second 10,000 catalogs is small when applied against the over-all cost of the catalog program, provided 20,000 are printed during one press set-up.

15. *Method of distribution.* The best way to deliver new catalogs is by the sales force. This provides salesmen with another opportunity to stand face-to-face with potential clients. Often there are just too many catalogs to be distributed. If this is the case, the mails become the most practical method of distribution. Person-to-person contact is lost when using the mails, and other means must be found to create interest in a company and its products. A premailing promotion campaign should be developed to announce the publication of the new catalog. An additional promotion piece published with the catalog distribution is equally important. The envelope used to mail the catalog should be carefully designed. Select an attention-attracting layout and be certain that the envelope clearly announces its contents.

16. *Advertising support.* Before the catalog is distributed it must be integrated into the over-all marketing and advertising plan. Advertising, catalogs, salesmen, and distributors are the basic marketing tools for selling products. Each of these can do part of the job, but for the most effective results they must be coordinated. A salesman's time is best used when he spends it talking to prospective clients who have been exposed to company advertisements or who have asked the salesman to call after seeing a product of interest in the catalog. Whenever practical, mention the catalog in advertisements. The entire sales force should be briefed on a new catalog. Catalog organization, new products, and so forth, should

be discussed. The salesmen must be thoroughly familiar with the contents and know how to find specific products in the least amount of time. If a salesman fumbles through a catalog to find a specific product in the presence of a potential client, the smooth sales presentation is broken and his chances of a sale dwindle. It is imperative that a catalog be integrated into the over-all market plan so that it can do the job for which it was designed.

3

COST ANALYSIS

This chapter discusses the first obstacle in a catalog program, the preparation and approval of the budget. It usually is not difficult to convince someone of the need for a catalog; however, when the same persons review the catalog budget, a sudden change of attitude occurs. Their reaction often can be anticipated. Why so much? This is the typical response someone unaware of the many processes necessary to produce a quality catalog. Some education on catalog preparation helps to avoid this reaction. Simply outline in the budget each activity or step that must be performed to prepare a catalog and put a price on each so that the budget reviewers can see where money is required.

When estimating costs, eliminate as much guesswork as possible. Printing, typography, and photography should be supported by written formal estimates from qualified suppliers. The tendency to prepare low budgets, thus providing a more attractive package for management approval, could be disastrous. Catalogs fall into the basic category of "you get what you pay for." Management must be convinced that catalog program costs are a selling investment, not just another overhead cost. As previously stated, many times your catalog is the only contact a potential client has with a company and its products. If it fails to tell the story, a sale is lost.

If a catalog is to perform as an effective selling tool, all phases of its preparation and production must be professionally initiated and executed. It is best to start with a sound budget prepared by experienced catalog people. If experienced personnel are not available in-house, ask a competent catalog agency for assistance in preparing a budget. This service is often provided by the catalog agency at no charge and under no obligation.

When preparing literature budgets, there are many factors often overlooked that can drastically affect your catalog costs. Those that should be considered are the following:

1. Cooperation
2. Approval authority
3. Accuracy of source data
4. Quality
5. Type of products
6. Status of products
7. Available literature
8. Special requirements
9. Schedule

1. *Cooperation.* Cooperation from all departments concerned with the catalog is essential. This must begin with the planning stage and continue through copy writing, photography, art preparation, and approvals. Without this cooperation your catalog production costs will mount and schedules will be missed. Many agencies admit that cooperation is the biggest single contributor to literature production cost. Many times it is difficult to predict cooperation because personalities are involved. List all personnel who contribute inputs to the catalog program and make mental notes of their work habits. Will they deliver on time? If not, contingencies must be allowed. "How much" must be determined by "how bad."

2. *Approval authority.* The number of people required to approve the catalog has a direct bearing on catalog production costs. More persons mean increased costs. This does not imply that having one man responsible for catalog approval produces the best catalog. On the contrary, catalogs should be approved by a committee. This is the most difficult method of getting approval, but the importance of a catalog justifies this inconvenience. A committee performs best when ruled by a competent chairman who is capable of filtering out trivial comments and acting on only the significant recommendations. A successful salesman should be given a voice in catalog approvals. Effective sales techniques should be studied and applied to the catalog presentation. Whether catalog approval is by committee or by one man, it is important that the chief copywriter and artist meet with the approval authority before copy or rough art is prepared. Agreement early in the preparation phase should reduce copy and art revisions.

3. *Accuracy of source data.* This point is self-explanatory; data must be accurate. If source data have not been finalized, additional time is required for thorough verification of all facts and statements. This is particularly important for the products' specifications and dimensions. Releas-

ing inaccurate data in a catalog creates customer ill will that could have been avoided. There is no way of determining how much harm is created by this avoidable nuisance.

4. *Quality.* During budget preparation some thought must be given to the quality of the catalog desired. The best is not always practical. Higher quality usually requires more time and better materials and greater costs. If circumstances do not permit the best, some compromises must be made. A delicate balance must be maintained so that the product is satisfactory and performs its function. In the chapters that follow shortcuts that do not seriously affect the over-all program are given. Now it is necessary to determine only the quality desired. Good is the minimum requirement; excellent is more desirable; and outstanding is the target.

5. *Type of products.* The level of catalog copy is determined by the product or system you are marketing. If it is unique, complicated, or technical, a writer or engineer who is technically competent must be assigned the copywriting task. If the subject matter is nontechnical and uncomplicated, a writer without an engineering background can be used. Usually writers with higher salaries are those with some engineering background. The important point is to match the proper writer to the product.

6. *Status of products.* Another factor that influences catalog costs is the status of products. New products often are affected by design changes that must be included in the catalog. New photographs must replace the obsolete. If up-to-date products are not immediately available, extensive airbrushing or new drawings may be necessary to give them proper coverage. Copy must be checked to evaluate the effect of product change.

7. *Available literature.* All available literature must be gathered and evaluated. If the material can be used as is, substantial savings are realized. If there are some changes, the copy should be verified to ensure that all changes are included. Any field comments that are available should be evaluated. If possible, all suggestions that help a product sell should be incorporated in the catalog. Savings can be obtained by selecting artwork used in the preparation of existing literature. This artwork should not be used if it is not compatible with other catalog illustrations. Remember, strive for a smooth presentation throughout the catalog. It cannot be obtained by combining many different types of illustrations. This subject is discussed in more detail in Chapter 7.

8. *Special requirements.* This item is mentioned because often during the catalog development someone wants to include information that does not belong. The justification offered is usually, "kill two birds with one stone," a very dangerous policy. Selling products is the function of a catalog; loading it down with unnecessary technical data and dissertations on company history decreases the catalog's usefulness because it

increases its size. If the catalog sells your product successfully, it has done its job. To try to do more can only hinder the ability of the catalog to perform its selling function.

9. *Schedule.* Establishing a workable schedule is one of the best methods of controlling spending for any program. This is particularly true of a catalog program. Is the catalog schedule realistic or must it be prepared on a crash basis? It is a fact that rushed jobs cost more. Setting realistic deadlines and having an effective follow-up system force decisions and keep the program moving toward completion. Extending deadlines causes delays and additional liaison. Disrupted schedules create many problems; problems create rising costs. It is essential that schedules be set and met to make a reasonably accurate budget prediction.

How much contingency should you allow for the nine points discussed? There is no existing formula to determine their effects. The estimator must depend on his company experience and particularly on the personalities of those who contribute to catalog preparation and approval.

A catalog agency is at a disadvantage in these areas. To combat this their representative, who in most cases prepares the budget proposal, should be thoroughly oriented. He should inquire about most or all of the nine points discussed. Answer his inquiries, for if an agency is to do a professional job, it must have complete cooperation. If a competent agency does a good job, you benefit; if it does a poor one, you lose. This does not mean that an agency proposal should be accepted without proper justification; it means that an agency budget reflects the quality of the product you have specified. If a lower price is desired, catalog quality must be reduced, either in preparation or printing.

Care must be exercised so that cost-estimating schemes do not become too involved. There is a point at which time or money become unnecessarily wasted if long complicated forms must be completed. A catalog program can be divided into four main phases—planning, manuscript and rough artwork, mechanicals, and production. Use this breakdown in the preparation of the catalog budget. Each of the phases is discussed.

Planning phase. The cost of planning begins the day the need for a new catalog is recognized. Activities to be completed in the planning phase include a field survey, catalog outline and specifications, budget, and the formation of the basic catalog team or the selection of a catalog agency. These activities are management functions. The direct contribution of management in terms of catalog pages published cannot be assessed and if it could would probably be a low percentage of the over-all program. Without good management the catalog program cannot avoid the many pitfalls present. As a rule, the actual cost of the planning phase should be approximately 15 percent of the over-all catalog program. To launch the catalog program a token budget should be established so that the activities in the planning phase can be completed. The second phase, preparation of manuscript and rough artwork, should not be started until all contributors understand what is expected of them. If there are areas of uncertainty, there should be discussions and warnings on potential budgets and schedule delays. Reshuffling budgets and schedules once the program has commenced diverts valuable production time. It is during the planning phase that the catalog coordinator assumes his responsibility.

Manuscript phase. The purpose of this phase is to complete a cohesive rough copy of the catalog. If possible, this should include preliminary layouts of each page or at least a representative layout of each type of page, such as straight text, tabular, and specifications. Departments requiring budget inputs in this phase include engineering, sales and marketing, advertising, and publications. The input from the engineering department is particularly important if products are complicated or technical. Enough engineering time must be given to help collect data, to answer all technical questions, and to approve the copy for technical accuracy. The sales and marketing department must provide some guidance toward the best sales appeal. It is in daily contact with clients and potential customers. It knows what questions are asked most about products and what information is needed. Sales and marketing must approve all manuscript copy. The advertising department also should be consulted. Catalog sales messages should conform to advertising sales messages. At this time the advertising department should start a campaign announcing the coming of the new catalog. The publications department normally would supply the copywriters, editors, artists, typists, and reproduction facilities. Larger companies may have a separate catalog department which would perform the functions just described for the publications department. The copywriters and artists must collaborate throughout the manuscript phase to produce the most effective product presentation. The artists need not be concerned with finished artwork at this point but should have sketches depicting intended artwork. During the manuscript phase, the artist should firm up format and type specifications. The supporting services, such as typing, proofreading, and reproduction, must be made available as needed.

The catalog coordinator is the person responsible for the successful completion of this phase. As previously stated, he must be thoroughly experienced with all the activities discussed. For large catalogs the coordinating effort is a full-time task. For smaller catalogs the coordinator should be capable of producing some of the copy. With his experience, he is in the best position to establish the budget within which he must operate. A summary of cost factors for the manuscript phase is given in Figure 8.

Department	Activity	Hours	Rate	Dollars
Engineering				
	Liaison			
	Copy approval			
Sales/marketing				
	Liaison			
	Copy approval			
Advertising				
	Consulting			
Publications or catalog				
	Catalog coordinator			
	Copy writer			
	Editor			
	Artist			
	Layout and type specification sketches			
	Typists			
	Proofreaders			
	Reproduction			
	Direct costs total			
	Overhead			
	Materials			
	TOTAL			

Figure 8.   Manuscript phase cost factors.

Mechanical phase. The preparation of printer's mechanicals should be started only after the manuscript has been approved by all departments concerned. Mechanicals are the finished reproducible copy used by the printer. If larger catalogs are divided into sections, the preparation of mechanicals could start after receipt of approval for each section. If there are references to other sections, they must be carefully noted and dropped in at a later date. This method keeps the program moving while waiting for approval of the remainder of the catalog. If any rewriting is necessary because of unclear review comments, it should be done immediately and resubmitted for approval before mechanical preparation begins. All photographs must be taken and artwork finalized, sized, and placed in proper positions. If prior approval is received on the suggested photographs, photography can begin before manuscript is formally approved. Again, this helps accelerate the program.

Final typography, whether hot or cold, is a time-consuming task which must be started as soon as possible. The layout artist should specify type for the manuscript and release the copy to the typesetter (hot composition) or typists (cold composition). After the mechanicals are built and all artwork is reduced and in place, a complete copy must be circulated for final approval. A summary of cost factors for the mechanical phase is given in Figure 9. Before continuing to the production phase, mention must be made of author's alterations (AAs). This is the name assigned to all changes after the page mechanicals are prepared. Changes made in this stage are very costly. Many author's alterations can be eliminated by a more thorough review of the manuscript. Author's alterations caused by equipment design unfortunately are cost factors that are difficult to predict. If these changes affect catalog information, mechanicals must be revised. Never publish data that is known to be wrong. If the catalog program is planned properly, author's alterations will normally not exceed 10 percent of the program cost. The catalog coordinator should be aware that author's alteration costs are potentially the most influential cost factor in the program. He must warn all personnel responsible for approving the manuscript of this cost factor and have all departments properly acknowledge approvals.

Production phase. The budget for the production phase should include costs of printing, binding, and distributing the catalog. Usually, it is most economical to find a supplier who will perform all these functions. Distribution after initial circulation is a cost that must be based on past catalog history. Check the records and determine how many catalog requests are received annually. It is good policy to order at least 10 percent

Department	Activity	Hours	Rate	Dollars
Engineering				
	Approval			
Marketing/Sales				
	Approval			
Advertising				
	Approval			
Publications or catalog				
	Catalog coordinator			
	Copy writer			
	Editor			
	Artist 　Type specification 　finished artwork			
	Typists (cold-type 　composition only)			
	Proofreaders (cold-type 　composition only)			
	Materials (stats, hot 　composition, illustra- 　tion board, and so 　forth)			
	Direct costs total			
	Overhead			
	Material handling			
	TOTAL			

Figure 9.   Mechanical preparation cost factors.

more printed catalogs than are actually required. The printing and binding costs of the extra quantity are trivial when compared with the total program cost. By doing this, a premature catalog reprint may be prevented. Remember when ordering catalog reprints that press set-up time must be paid again, thus increasing the unit cost of a printed catalog.

All estimated prices from suppliers should be formalized or confirmed. When obtaining prices, give suppliers as much information as possible. A large factor in printing prices is finding a printer with the right equipment for your job. Get competitive bids from at least three printers. Any bid that is substantially lower than the others should be carefully reviewed and evaluated before it is entered in your budget. Printers can make errors; have the low bidder recheck his figures. This may prevent problems later.

Throughout this section no actual dollars have been mentioned. Generalizing estimating catalog costs is almost impossible. For this reason this chapter offers guides rather than rules to determine pricing. For more accurate predictions each program must be judged on its individual merits and factors. Generally, the per page price range from catalog agencies is $150 to $250 per mechanical. This does not include the production phase. The $100 per page price span gives some idea how various weighing factors can influence catalog costs.

When presenting the complete budget for approval, use the basic breakdown discussed. Put prices on each phase. This provides an opportunity to acquaint management with the many difficult activities required to prepare a catalog. If cuts must be made, management must decide where the compromise is to be made. If you are shortchanged, be sure that management is aware of the effects the budget cuts will have on the published catalogs. Catalogs can be prepared on limited budgets. Unless there is a captive clientele, this normally means limited results.

4

COPY PREPARATION

Before writing the first manuscript copy, the catalog coordinator must organize all available material and develop the catalog team. At this time a thorough review of the catalog purpose, reader, general outline, and so forth is essential. Plans should be made to develop a detailed and specific outline. Additional research for facts and figures must be made. When gathering data, always keep a good set of notes on your research. Once enough information is available a through breakdown of the catalog can be made. This should include specific wording for headings, subheadings, and sub-subheadings. When this task is completed, the basic organization of the catalog is clearly revealed. Plans for a good indexing system can be explored when the specific outline is complete. Do not begin copywriting the first draft until the subject matter has been researched and the specific outline is complete.

Before discussing copywriting, the prerequisites of a copywriter are examined. What makes a good copywriter? The capacity to communicate effectively by the written word is one of the most sought after skills in industry today. A person who can write clearly, correctly, and concisely is more valuable than the individual who has never learned to express himself effectively. Modern business cannot operate economically without effective oral and written communications. Many imaginative ideas are lost through the inability to communicate them. Any intelligent person who conscientiously applies himself can learn to write.

Catalog copywriting and other forms of literature have many things in common. Both are concerned with grammar, punctuation, spelling, abbreviations, organization, logical development of thought, paragraphing, and so forth. These subjects are rather fundamental, and many good reference books are available on them. There are, however, other considerations that are more important in a catalog than in other forms of literature.

In catalog copy accuracy is most important. All information must be exact. Incorrect information can cause a client to make a wrong choice when ordering. There is no excuse that will erase the ill will caused by this situation. Thus inaccuracies that may be considered of minor consequence in other forms of writing cannot be tolerated in a sales catalog.

Catalog copy must be clear to the user. Clarity involves vocabulary level, exactness of words, logical development of thoughts, and simple sentence structure. Always use the same product name throughout the copy; for example, when discussing covers, do not call them covers in one portion of copy and lids in the next. Application of this simple rule makes your message clearer.

Conciseness is another noteworthy characteristic that is desirable in catalog copy. It helps the user to obtain information faster and more easily. Conciseness is obtained by various methods, including the elimination of repetition, the deletion of nonessential material, avoidance of lengthy phrases and complicated sentence structure, and the intelligent use of complementing tables, graphs, and illustrations.

The greatest difference between catalog copywriting and other forms of copywriting is the tone or slant of the messages. Catalog copy must do two things, tell and sell. How is this done? Place yourself in the buyer's position. Why does he buy? Usually he buys to obtain some form of benefit. Benefit is the key word; the benefits that can be gained by the purchaser must be emphasized in catalog copy. Positive statements of benefits should be supported by tangible proof, such as specifications (for more technical products) and pictures (for more domestic products).

The remainder of this chapter discusses successful techniques for producing good catalog copy, from the gathering of data through illustration planning.

GATHERING SOURCE MATERIAL

If the copywriter is familiar with the subject matter, there is a dangerous tendency that he will develop a casual attitude, a feeling of being at home with the subject. If this is the case, he tends to believe that his knowledge of the subject is enough. This is not true. His knowledge can be beneficial, but it must be supplemented by other inputs and the marketing message (the sell portion) must be clear.

Conferences are probably the best and fastest method of collecting data. They should be tape recorded so that the copywriter can review the conference discussions. Conferences usually raise important points from personal experiences that must be carefully evaluated. The human element makes a person stress his own experience and de-emphasize areas or products about which he knows little. Products should be given proportionate treatment. Do not "ride" the big seller at the expense of products that are as important to sell. If they were unimportant, their manufacture could not be justified.

Conduct conferences for source-gathering material as you would a personal interview. Listed below are typical questions that, if answered, will give a solid basis for copywriting. The list does not apply to all products and is intended only as a guide.

1. What is the official name of the product?
2. What are the product's benefits?
3. What are the specific models, units, grades, or brands?
4. Is the product's name registered?
5. Does the product conform to any generally known code, standard, or specification?
6. What are typical and potential uses of the product?
7. What are its limitations?
8. How is it installed and what are the essential dimensions?
9. How easy is it to operate?
10. What textures and colors are available?
11. How much does it weigh and how is it normally shipped?
12. What are the pertinent mechanical, environmental, and electrical specifications?
13. What maintenance support and services are available?
14. Is the product usually stocked?
15. What is a normal delivery period?
16. Should prices be included and what are they?
17. Are all sales representatives and distributors briefed on the product?

Another available avenue for obtaining information is reviewing all literature. This includes competitors' literature. Regardless of how thoroughly a subject is known, all existing sources of information must be researched. Evaluate all printed sources; read everything available on the subject; learn as much as possible and be prepared to ask intelligent, meaningful questions during conference interviews. Often, studying the approaches used in available literature inspires new ideas for more effective presentations. Objectively written matter, untinged by personal feelings, provides the best source information. It helps to increase knowledge so that propet weight and proportion is given to all subjects. Expertise must be established before it is possible to write the most effective copy.

A note of caution must be given; having vast amounts of data does not guarantee good copy. Screen your sources; filter out all extraneous matter. Condensation of all the source information collected into good catalog copy is the most difficult and important function of the copywriter.

BASIC COPYWRITING GUIDES

Generally, a potential customer has a specific need in mind when he picks up a catalog. Product selection to satisfy this need is usually based on appearance, function, quality, availability, and price. It is only natural that a potential customer should hope to find information on each basic characteristic so that an intelligent selection can be made easily. If information is lacking in any area, the user may write for additional information (if you are fortunate). He may also not bother any further, make a wrong assumption, or worst of all, go to a competitor's catalog. Each of the basic needs is discussed separately.

Appearance

If your product is a visual element in a home, office, or factory, it will not sell unless the potential buyer is favorably impressed by its appearance. Although the copywriter has no control over the physical appearance of a product, he does exercise control over its presentation in the catalog. Remember how extremely sensitive people are to appearance. This characteristic can be used to advantage by slanting copy toward the appearance of products.

Function

All potential buyers want to know how a product will benefit them. Much of the art of copywriting is in knowing how to prepare copy for many persons that seems to be a personal message prepared especially for one. This is why it is important to know as much about a potential buyer as possible. Most products are used by a general class or category of people who have a language and a point of view peculiarly their own. Copy produces the best results when it is written in the right language or tone and expresses the reader's point of view.

Quality

The quality of a product must be reflected in the quality of catalog presentation. Most persons are visually-minded by nature, experience, environment, and training; therefore they are highly perceptive and critical of catalog presentation. In professional presentations the most likely conclusion is that the catalog supports top-notch products. Spare no effort to show by the quality of the catalog the excellence of the products. The power of suggestion, if used properly, produces desired results.

If products are technical, their quality is best shown by including specifications, diagrams, graphs, tables, and outline drawings. Many technically-inclined persons want the facts so they can draw their own conclusions. Writing copy for engineers that tells them how good a product is becomes a waste of time and effort unless the copy is supported by specific data and test results. If many inquiries are received by the sales department for more technical information, it indicates that more specific data are needed in your catalog.

Availability

Immediate availability of products is one of the best selling features often overlooked in copywriting. Remember there is a need for your product; this is why it is selected from the catalog. The sooner that need is satisfied, the more pleased the client is. Positive statements, such as "immediately available" or "off-the-shelf item," help sell. Use them whenever possible. If a product is not immediately available, some statement should be included to indicate availability. If the purpose of the catalog is not to sell directly, clear, positive steps must be given to the user. Let him know of the company's interest in him and stand ready to service him promptly. The company has gone to great expense and trouble to arouse interest in its products, do not obstruct the sales effort at this stage. Smooth the buyer's way toward calling a sales representative or specification writer by telling him where and how personnel can be reached.

Price

Whenever practical, price information should be given. This saves numerous, time-consuming inquiries. Generally, no product or service is sold without some form of financial agreement being established first. When specific pricing information cannot be included in a catalog, consideration should be given to providing at least some indication of cost, in terms of other similar products or comparative price ranges. When applicable, long-term costs, such as maintenance or service contracts, should be included.

When the source-gathering and basic research phases are complete, again check the detailed outline thoroughly and fill any obvious gaps.

The detailed outline is the catalog plan developed to guide manuscript writing in order to produce a coherent, smooth-flowing draft. Writing assignments can be made using the outline, thus giving all contributors a clear understanding of where their contribution fits into the over-all picture. By using a working outline, copywriting need not start with the first topic in the catalog. Remember, starting at the beginning is not always the best procedure for copywriters. This may seem unusual, but writing is a job that often reflects personal traits. Some copywriters may have difficulty getting started. This problem can be alleviated by assigning them a section that is easier or one with which they are most familiar. The best example of this is writing the catalog introduction. It is strongly recommended that the catalog introduction be written last. A good introduction is an integral part of the catalog, not just a skipped-over foreword that obviously has been written as an afterthought. It should arouse the user's interest, explain the purpose of the catalog, and give the basic plan of presentation and instructions on the best way to use the catalog.

When preparing copy, the writer should remember that facts alone do not make a manuscript coherent. Even if the facts are presented orderly, a reader must be led smoothly from one topic to another in a way that will not confuse him. To maintain continuity, not only in catalog copywriting but in all forms of writing, there are many techniques that can be employed. The most important is smooth transition. Smooth transition helps bridge annoying gaps between segments of writing, such as sentence parts, whole sentences, paragraphs, sections, and chapters. Each sentence within a paragraph or piece of copy should be related in some way to the previous thought and lead into what follows; otherwise the writing becomes jumbled, disassociated, and incoherent. '

A writer has many transitional words at his disposal. The use of these words helps him show an addition, contrast, exception, contradiction, or summary, all of which help to bridge the gaps and tie the sales message together. Transition between sentences is only the first step toward giving copy continuity. Although sentences are the basic building blocks, they must be grouped into expressive paragraphs with messages that the reader can grasp easily.

The conventional definition of a paragraph, a group of sentences relate to one idea or with related thoughts, must be adjusted to the capabilities and limitations of the intended reader and the material presented. For instance, paragraphs containing technical information should be much shorter than paragraphs containing less technical material. A reader must concentrate more on technical information. By breaking the presentation down into smaller segments, the pauses needed for copy to be absorbed and understood are built-in. Although one generally reads sentences, attention is focused on the paragraph; therefore if paragraphs are too long, pertinent relationships are confused and the full impact of the message is lost.

Paragraphs must be planned properly and written skillfully if total communication between reader and writer are to be established. Although the catalog language is marketing-oriented, the standard practices for writing good paragraphs in English composition must be applied.

* All paragraphs should have topic sentences.
* All sentences in the paragraph should be related to the topic.
* Smooth transitions are necessary between successive sentences.
* All paragraphs should end with some form of summary device.

The discussion on paragraphing is not intended to be an endorsement of lengthy copy. The most effective sales copy is brief. Long-winded copy which demands too much concentration will tire the reader and cause him to lose interest. Again there is a delicate balance that must be maintained. Give the reader enough information to tell the complete story without the copy becoming lengthy, cumbersome, and boring.

In summary keep copy cohesive; make the material cling together. Use a beginning that attracts the reader and leads smoothly into the main message. Be sure all material is both pertinent and interesting.

Writing Style

Much has been written about writing style. The most basic rule is to write copy as though one is talking directly to the reader. This is why one must know and anticipate the reader. Although the tone of catalog copy should be conversational, word selection should be precise and exacting. If copy is vague, general, or not in context with the reader's vocabulary, the sales message loses effectiveness. Remember, no matter how well the subject is known or investigated, efforts are wasted if the reader does not understand or is confused by the material. Remember also that this is usually not a captive audience. There may be only one chance; make the best of it by presenting the most effective sales message.

Copy should go from general to specific whenever possible. If only general facts of statements are given, they should be supported by at least one example. As a rule, readers find it hard to understand generalities unless specific examples are given.

Writing style also encompasses readability. Again, many articles and books have been written on guides toward good, readable copy. What makes copy readable? Readable copy has the right words arranged in sentences and paragraphs that are appealing, informative, direct, and clear. A readable style is something that is developed through trial and error by writing, revising, and rewriting. Because the catalog is important, catalog copy should not be written by writer trainees who are still developing a readable style.

Word selection is a major factor that determines copy readability. Choosing the right word for the right place is a key function of the writer. Select words that are most familiar to your reader. If possible, use concrete words in place of abstract words and action verbs instead of verbs that indicate state, mood, or condition.

Another factor that makes catalog copy more readable is the use of personal pronouns. Normally, a writer leaves "I" out of copy because it identifies him too closely; this identification gives an opinionated slant to an otherwise objective presentation. The use of the pronouns "we" and "you," however, often helps to get the reader interested. Do not overuse them. The pronoun "we" can be used to suggest cooperative ventures between reader and writer, whereas the pronoun "you" leads to reader participation. Many writers use the pronoun "you" too frequently in their efforts to communicate with the reader. It is often more effective to imply "you" than to use it.

Illustrations and First Draft

Although the primary subject of this chapter is writing copy, some mention of illustrations must be made. Good illustrations can enhance any literature and this certainly applies to a catalog. Illustrations must appear throughout and be carefully planned. Writers and artists must work together and pool their efforts to produce the most effective presentation. This togetherness must start at the rough-draft stage. Do not wait until there is a finished manuscript before planning illustrations. Integrate them into the copy as it is prepared. The illustrations should be positioned as closely to the related text as possible. Do not leave it up to the catalog user to relate text and illustrations. If figure references are necessary, use them. If the illustration is immediately adjacent to its related text, references may not be necessary. If captions are necessary, be concise.

The type of illustration that is to be prepared is as important as its position in relation to the copy. It may appear to be a little early to be worrying about illustrations, but illustration availability must be determined as soon as possible. If photographs are to be taken, the exact equipment must be available. If this is not possible, a suitable compromise must be made. Photographs add more impact to a catalog than any other type of illustration and they prove the physical existence of your product. Line renderings suggest that your product is still on the drawing board. Photographs of an actual installation that clearly show your equipment should be used when applicable.

There are other illustrations besides photographs that can provide marketing value. Installation and outline drawings often are not only helpful but necessary. A wiring or schematic diagram that illustrates easy installation or clearly shows a specific technical point can be used. There is no limit to the type of illustrations that should be used. Any that best point out a pertinent idea or thought that could help sell your product should be used. The different types of illustration are discussed in Chapter 7.

Illustrations

The proper type and correct placement of illustrations are not a guarantee that a reader will study them. Refer to the illustration in the copy at the precise moment that you want the reader to look at it. The reference should imply "look at the illustration right now." In some cases refer to an illustration by its page placement: above, below, here, and so forth. Be sure the reference is properly marked so that the layout artist is warned; otherwise the illustration may be placed incorrectly and the reference will be useless and confusing. The reference should not be left out of the copy and put in later by the layout artist because this creates a more difficult problem; that is, finding room for a reference sentence. Put the reference in at the draft stage and clearly flag it.

Make sure you get the maximum benefit from an illustration. Talk about it. Tell the reader why the illustration is in the catalog. Tell him to notice something specific and point out equipment features from which he will benefit. Do not expect that a single illustration reference will make the reader see everything you want. Take the initiative by mentioning all items of interest.

Some thought must be given to the final size of the illustrations in the printed catalog. In some cases you may wish to reduce an existing drawing to fit a particular space. Many times reducing or enlarging an illustration makes little difference in legibility. This should be checked with your artist or production man, for if the illustration is complicated or has labeled callouts, it will not be effective in the catalog if it is too small. An illustration, such as a graph, which is reduced too much and becomes difficult to read and understand is not worth including.

Consider the reader when preparing illustrations: label parts when necessary, keep the illustration simple, use a clear caption, and reproduce it legibly.

A copywriter should prepare specifications for every illustration in the catalog. This may be in the form of a picture cutout from an existing brochure or old catalog with new instructions or a note to print as is. Do not leave it entirely up to the artist to produce the illustrations you want. Give him detailed instructions when they are needed; usually he can follow any reasonable instructions. If the illustration is technical the artist may require more information. Work with him and solicit his suggestions for improvements. It is sometimes helpful for the artist to read copy so he clearly understands the point to be illustrated. He may even spot areas in the copy that may benefit from an illustration that was overlooked.

At this stage some thought must be given to the use of color. In many cases color is needed. A catalog should have at least one color in addition to the basic black. Color, when properly used, makes illustrations more effective. It can also be used to clarify graphs or to produce a standardized appearance or format throughout the catalog. Some warning should be given, however; do not use a great many colors in an illustration just to make it more attractive. This type of presentation is for advertisements not for catalogs. A flashy illustration is used for an eye-catcher and belongs in your advertising. The same illustration in a catalog has initial appeal, but if the catalog is designed for longevity flashy illustrations reduce its useful life.

The addition of color adds to cost, time, and trouble; therefore unless it helps the reader to provide a better means of getting a point across, do not use it. When additional colors are planned, have a specific function for them. If there are legitimate reasons for a multicolored catalog, do not hesitate to use additional colors. With them, the artist can skillfully apply all tricks of the trade to make them most effective. When you are planning to use additional colors, the importance of writer and artist coordination increases.

PRODUCING THE FIRST MANUSCRIPT

The completion of a rough manuscript draft is a major milestone in a catalog program. Before circulating the draft, it should be checked by a qualified editor. Regardless of how much effort was spent in its preparation, the rough draft almost always needs editing and revision. During the editing function, the draft should be checked not only for spelling, punctuation, and grammatical errors, but also should be appraised for over-all content, approach, and presentation. An experienced editor can determine these points because he is trained to visualize or project the appearance of the material in its final form.

The catalog has a particular need to fill. The copywriter knows the catalog objectives before he writes the first word; he investigates these objectives during the planning phase. Now that the draft is written, an editor must judge whether the writer has produced the copy that will successfully attain the catalog objectives. The copy has a job to perform; it must give potential customers specific facts about your products; it must emphasize all major areas and include minor details only when they are absolutely necessary. The material must be orderly and presented in proper sequence.

It is a mistaken belief that the first stream of thoughts is always the best. A catalog is too important to include anything but the best. When a competent editor reviews a draft, he combines fresh imagination with deliberate thinking. Usually, the edited results are more smooth and have unity, coherence, and proper emphasis. These are notable characteristics that help the catalog perform more effectively. Any unclear areas should be discussed with the copywriter and improved. The draft is now ready to be submitted for approval by the designated authorities. If the edited draft is marked heavily, it should be retyped before submission.

An important point that will save costs should be injected here. If the final copy is to be typeset, the draft should be prepared from non-proportional spaced machines. This makes character counting, a function required during copyfitting, easier. Character counting is discussed further in Chapter 6.

COPY APPROVAL AND FOLLOW-UP

If close coordination between copywriters and approval agents is maintained during copy preparation, approval comments should be minimized. If the approval review is performed by several reviewers, the copywriter must combine all necessary comments into a final manuscript. This task is performed best with all people concerned present at a reviewer's conference. This is not always possible so it is the writer's task to make certain that all approval agents are aware of all comments.

If the writer thinks that a suggested change contains an error or introduces confusion or complications, he must discuss the matter further with the reviewer before going ahead and incorporating it. Although an approval agent's comments are normally mandatory, they should not be taken for granted.

In the comments the reviewer might ask the writer to verify the accuracy of certain information; if so, the writer must check back to the source and thoroughly research for possible errors. The reviewer might indicate that certain passages be rewritten or amplified; if so, the writer first must try to understand the reason for the criticism. Once this becomes apparent, the right slant on the new copy should be obvious. Depending on the extent of the rewrite the copy may have to be submitted again for proper approval.

When incorporating review comments or making other changes, the copywriter must be extremely careful to avoid the introduction of new errors. The most vulnerable areas are page and figure references. If pages or figures have been added or deleted, the entire numbering sequence following the change is upset; therefore the manuscript must be thoroughly screened for references. In larger catalogs an index of references should be made. This will facilitate changes made at a later date.

After all manuscript changes have been made, the editor should read the entire copy. During this final check the editor may discover an error or vague area that was not previously noted. All references should be rechecked during this time.

In summary the preparation of copy is the real blood, tears, and sweat period for the writer. If he applies himself conscientiously during this time, he will be rewarded later by seeing his manuscript blossom into an effective printed catalog. This is the most satisfying experience an author can have, for to be a good writer you must take pride in your work. Pride is the ingredient that often makes the difference between a good job and the best job.

SPECIFICATION WRITING

Never in our history has the need for better specification writing been more important. This is dramatically evident when comparing the engineering talent available today with the needs of continuously expanding industry. Deciding what to include in specifications, how to state them, and what to leave out are among the most difficult problems of catalog preparation. These problems are compounded by the competitive atmosphere in which each manufacturer is trying to be honest, even conservative, yet trying to make his products look better on paper than his competitor's.

Total dollars spent in the last five years in the construction field alone staggers the imagination. Even more things are planned in the immediate future. What does this have to do with catalogs? In many technical and construction markets buying is influenced strongly by having a product specified or included in the original planning or proposal. The catalog can help by providing guide forms for specifying your product. The specification might be only a few words, in which case it would be contained on the page displaying the product for which it is used. It could also be many pages, and a separate section of the catalog could be allocated for it. The wording and phrasing in specification statements should be as precise, direct, and formal as possible. "Flowery" language has no application in specification writing.

What exactly is a specification? A specification is a statement of work or a contract that clearly and accurately details the requirements for a material, product, or service. The specification terms are usually written by the buyer and accepted by the seller. Specifications are usually supplemented by plans or drawings that together depict a proposed solution to a particular problem. Specifications unite the technical concepts of the engineer with the skilled hands of the contractor. They establish targets for basic standards of performance which must be equaled or exceeded if the desired results are to be obtained. They need not tell how the results are to be obtained but rather may detail the results. There are exceptions to this, particularly in the construction field. A general rule is that specifications should not limit the freedom of the contractor in his construction methods except where his methods may be detrimental to obtaining the proper results.

Are all specifications basically alike? No, there are three types of specifications—open, restricted, and closed.

Open Specifications

Open specifications are probably the most familiar. They are often called performance specifications. Military specifications are good examples of this type. The printing specifications that must be prepared to obtain quotations on printing services is another good example. As the name implies, open specifications are "open" to all manufacturers or suppliers in the field. The daily newspapers carry open specification listings which solicit bids. This is particularly true of federal and state government contracts that are normally required by law to use open specifications.

Open specifications for equipment are difficult to prepare. Many times, after the specification requirements are established, some suppliers are eliminated without a product actually being named simply because of certain limitations of their products. Although open specifications usually result in broader competition, they restrict control over specific product selection. Open specifications would not be used in a catalog for the requirements are too broad. If specifications are included, they would most likely be the restricted or closed types discussed below. The above discussion is given only to make the distinctions among the three specification categories clearer.

Restricted Specifications

A restricted specification gives not only the desired performance standards but goes one step further and mentions suppliers by name along with part or catalog numbers. Obviously, a catalog will not be published with specifications that include a competitor's name and product. The customary method employed for bypassing this problem is to list the catalog number and add either "or equal" or "or approved equal." There is a very important distinction between these two phrases. Using "or equal" means the contractor or consulting engineer will or should accept the supplier's statement that a substituted product is equal in performance to the specified product. Using "or approved equal," however, means any substituted product must have prior approval before it is considered acceptable. Also, some burden of proof is usually placed on the manufacturer of the substituted product; for example, several sets of working or shop drawings are often requested at least two weeks prior to the scheduled date for opening of bids. This time allows the engineer or architect to evaluate the substituted product. Some statement on cost differentials is also usually requested. In the statement any cost savings or increases should be clearly delineated.

Engineers generally prefer the restricted specification for most work done for private industry. This permits a reasonable amount of competition among contractor, supplier, and manufacturer while it gives the engineering authority some idea of what the final selection will be. Restrictive specifications are impractical for highly technical or extremely complicated systems, products, or materials.

Contractors usually prefer restricted specifications for they know exactly what products will be accepted; open specifications force them to make decisions that could be costly. Restricted specifications place the responsibility for equipment, system, or product performance standards with whom it belongs, the specifying engineer. When a contractor suggests a substitute, engineers immediately become suspicious. In most instances substitutes suggested by contractors are influenced primarily by a price advantage. The engineer must make certain that the contractor is not substituting price for quality. His evaluation should be tempered by the courage of his convictions not by his stubbornness. If the substituted product is proven equal to or better than that specified, the engineer should accept it without further considerations.

Closed Specifications

Closed specifications mean exactly what the name implies. Specific products identified by manufacturer and catalog numbers are used. At first glance it may appear that all competitive advantages are lost. If the specifications are prepared properly, this is not so. A closed specification is usually prepared after either an open or restrictive specification was submitted for quotations. After quotations are received, the engineer can rewrite the specification using the items he thinks are best suited to his needs. This puts the responsibility for the entire selection of equipment on the engineer. Because the engineer is acting as the buyer's agent, the responsibility is properly designated. This should provide the buyer with better engineering at a lower cost. Design changes late in a building program should almost be eliminated. There are many persons involved in transactions requiring specification writing; a closed specification places all persons in proper perspective.

Many contractors frown on closed specifications. They are given limited room to shop for price because the product has already been specified by catalog number. This means that material costs for all competing contractors will be equal or nearly equal; therefore the only way he can underbid other contractors is to provide more efficient labor. Again, the buyer benefits. One advantage the contractor has with closed specifications is that he cannot be held responsible for performance or be liable for guarantees. Obviously he must accept responsibility for the quality of his workmanship.

The language of the specifications, no matter what type, should be as firm as the convictions of the specifying engineer. If he is confident that he is specifying the best equipment, he should be firm and allow no substitutes.

Influencing Factors of Product Selection

There are many factors that an engineer must evaluate before selecting a product for the specification. The more he knows about these factors, the better equipped he is to present facts about each. Some of the most important factors are listed below:

1. Capabilities and limitations
2. Price
3. Manufacturer's reputation
4. Availability of engineering information
5. Delivery
6. Past or current performances

Using Existing Specification Standards

There are many recognized organizations and agencies that have specification standards. Typical organizations are the National Electrical Manufacturers Association, the National Board of Five Underwriters, the American Society for Testing Materials, and the American Standards Association. Their standards, when applicable to your product, should be used to ensure clear, concise, specification wording. Adoption of a recognized standard eliminates excessive verbiage and provides comprehensive coverage. The National Electric Code is often referenced in specifications for electronic and electrical devices. Specific paragraph numbers can be used to make the specification more concise. The engineer responsible for specification writing should be aware of all applicable standard specifications and make liberal use of them. He must also be aware of state and local codes that may define restrictions or refinements peculiar to a particular locale. These must be included in plans and specifications to avoid costly changes later in the program.

Typical Guide-Form Specifications

When applicable, guide-form specifications should be included to provide an aid for preparing specifications. Obviously, these specifications should be slanted toward your products. Providing guide-form specifications makes it easier for the engineer to specify a product. The most important function of a catalog is to make it easy for potential customers to buy or specify products. In many markets the first step toward a sale is the specification. Keep the guide-form specifications simple and include standard products. This will give you a price advantage when it is time for product purchasing.

It is difficult to provide a typical guide-form specification that applies to all situations. For simple items a brief statement often suffices. A typical specification statement may be, "Lumination shall be supplied by eight, 150-watt, soft-glow lamps (120 volts) made by the XYZ Company." More complex equipment will have specifications that include:

1. Statement of work
2. Standard products
3. Operation
4. Materials
5. Installation

The statements for each category must be clear and concise. Although specifications are considered legal documents, they should not be loaded with legal jargon. The quality of products should be reflected clearly in guide-form specifications. Be as straightforward about specification statements as possible.

The Importance of Being Specified

Strong buying influences are exerted in drawings, plans, and specifications; therefore helping an architect or engineer to prepare a specification written about a product is an important first step. This does not necessarily assume a sale for last-minute changes is a common event that must be accepted. A good follow-up system, after products have been specified, is most important. Again, this emphasizes the importance of a complete marketing plan.

5

CATALOG DESIGN

In the preceding chapter procedures for making a more effective catalog with good copywriting are discussed. Such efforts will not be completely successful unless they are presented adequately in the catalog. In other words, good copywriting alone cannot do the job; neither will good illustrations by themselves give satisfactory results. In the final analysis the effectiveness of the catalog depends on how it is designed, visualized, laid out, and printed.

Many people think that once the copy is written the catalog is almost finished. There is a strong tendency to underestimate the work required for makeup, visualization, composition, preparation of final illustrations, and reproduction. This tendency is probably responsible for printer's copy being called "mechanicals." Makeup consists of assembling all page elements into their proper relationships. This means allowing the right amount of space for copy, art, running heads, folios, and captions on the page and positioning each to produce the best presentation.

THE FUNCTION OF THE ARTIST

In catalog development an important function of the artist is to create the best methods of interpreting and indicating the function of the catalog. The interpretation must be accurate, interesting, and pleasing. Both the type of composition and the artwork have character which, if used properly will develop a consistent mood to help the interpretation. Whether simple or complicated, character can be expressed in visual abstract terms. The artist must be thoroughly familiar with all the mechanics necessary to develop character.

The artist is sometimes known as a visualizer, layout man, illustrator, or makeup man. No matter what the title, he must be familiar with the contents of the copy, know the ultimate purpose of the catalog, know who will use it and how, and recognize the level of potential user. He cannot stop at giving only casual consideration to these factors for the results reflect how well he understood the precise message intended. Each important factor is reviewed from the artist's point of view.

Copy Familiarization

Before the artist can visualize he must become familiar with the contents of the copy. He must read the complete manuscript to learn as much as possible about the subject matter. Often, he will get helpful suggestions by studying the writing style, its approach to the subject, and the treatment that the copywriter gives it. If the copy is technical or complicated, a formal tone must be reflected in the presentation; on the other hand, the less formal copy in a domestic catalog permits more casual treatment of catalog appearance.

The artist need not read the copy to become expert in the subject, but he should know enough to converse intelligently with the writer and editor. No one can tell an artist how he should acquaint himself with the content of the copy. This is a more personal trait that depends on how the artist prefers to work. Certainly, the more he learns about the copy the better prepared he will be to produce the best treatment. Treatment applies not only to illustrations but to page layout, column width, folios, and other mechanics that are discussed later in this chapter. The final results of the artist's performance are judged by catalog users.

Catalog Purpose

Both the writer and editor must know the purpose of the catalog; so must the artist. He must create methods of motivating catalog users to buy products. As previously stated, the purpose of a catalog falls into one of three general categories: (a) sale by direct order from the catalog, (b) sale by having a salesman or representative call, and (c) sale by writing a product or system specification. The purpose of the catalog helps the artist to determine the best tone for visual treatment, for, although the catalog motive is to sell, the approaches used for soft sell versus hard sell should be different.

Catalog User

Again, the artist as well as the writer and editor must know the catalog user. This seems to overlap the catalog purpose, but there is no need to make a distinction. The important point is that the artist know the group of people the catalog is attempting to reach. He must use this gauge to determine proper treatment. The artist saves much time and effort by discussing this point with the writer. The writer, more than anyone, should be able to define clearly potential users. Making a study of them is a prerequisite for the writer. If he did not make the study, the sales program would be better if the catalog were not printed because a catalog's primary purpose is to pass sales information to potential clients. The catalog will do the best job only if it is written and presented in a way that is understood clearly by its users and will effect user behavior to advantage.

FUNCTIONAL DESIGN

At this stage of the catalog program the artist must develop a functional design that obtains the desired results. There are three basic steps toward providing the best functional design: (a) problem analysis, (b) evaluation of all possible solutions, and (c) selection of the best solution.

In the preceding paragraphs the items that must be analyzed are discussed. The primary reason for preliminary analysis is to form a good basis for future decisions. Designing a catalog is not a matter of doing everything at once. Instead, it is a gradual process of specific, orderly steps toward producing the best arrangement. Experienced design artists usually shorten the time span between the analysis phase and the selection of the best solution.

The solution or treatment selected must be consistent throughout each section of the catalog—the cover, front matter, index, and body. Each of these components is discussed separately.

Cover

The most important design consideration for the cover is that it is compatible with the cover material. The artist must know or evaluate the limitations of the material (paper, cloth, plastic, or leather). The best design is useless if it cannot be properly reproduced on the cover material. There are two basic points that should always be present on a catalog cover, company identification and product identification. The company identification should include a logo, name, and address. The product identification should be the product name or category. Some form of graphic representation such as a product photo, interesting cutaway view, or typical installation scheme that sets off the product is preferable. Covers for general catalogs can use a montage of products or simply state that it is a general catalog.

Another useful item that should be considered for inclusion on the cover is a catalog number. This is particularly important if there are several catalogs in the field. The catalog number serves as a quick reference which can be used to determine whether it is up-to-date.

Often, a company has a summary statement, such as "The oldest," "The largest," that it uses and is recognized in the field. The designer can make good use of this statement on the cover design.

A second color is a necessity on the cover, although there have been trends toward all white covers in an attempt to obtain distinction. The use of a second color also provides distinction. Remember, your catalog could be resting on a shelf with many others. Having a distinctive cover makes it stand out. A careful balance must be retained, because a too flashy color loses its effectiveness quickly.

Do not forget the cover spine. The spine is the part of the catalog that normally shows from the bookcase. It should identify the company and, if possible, the catalog products. This helps to distinguish your catalog from all others.

Front-Matter Pages

The design of the pages that comprise the front matter is determined mainly by the treatment of the rest of the catalog. If a definite design philosophy has been determined, it must be reflected on these pages. Basic catalog front-matter pages include a title page, warranty or guaranty page, foreword, contents, introduction, and company profile. This sequence is the most popular, but it can be modified to fit any circumstance. Each page of the front matter must be given careful consideration, no matter how unimportant it may seem to be. Each front-matter page is discussed separately.

Title Page. The title page is the entry to the catalog. It should be interesting and reveal the contents of the catalog. The title page should repeat all the cover information. In addition it should be dated. The title page must blend with all pages that follow. In effect the title page introduces the catalog's character to the user; therefore it cannot be an individual piece but must harmonize with the contents. There is a strong tendency to create abstract productions while totally ignoring all other factors. To avoid this pitfall develop the title-page design with several typical catalog pages in view.

Catalog title pages should always be right-hand pages. It is a fact that at the beginning of any book, the right-hand pages are the most prominent. Two-page spread title pages are not recommended for a catalog; they can increase production costs because exacting registration is necessary. They should be avoided.

When a second color is available it should be included in the design. This helps the title page harmonize with the catalog format. Color can be used to establish emphasis that otherwise would not be possible. It can be used for the title, a bar, a pattern, or a ghost, if desired. When using color on the title page, it must be consistent with color usage throughout the catalog. Strive for unity and coherence. Be certain there is a good reason for the use of color whenever it is applied. When choosing colors from a swatch book, remember that large areas appear lighter in color than small ones. This is particularly true if thin type is used in the title and the title is printed in color. Type in color appears thinner than type in black. To compensate for this a darker color must be used to keep the proper contrast.

The inside front cover that normally faces the title page could contain the standard "Copyright" and "Printed in U.S.A." notices. When material is copyrighted, exclusive rights to the contents of the printed matter are granted by law. All reproduction rights are reserved. The "Printed in U.S.A." notice is required when printed material is to be distributed outside the United States. Adding the notice provides a safeguard against this eventuality.

Warranty or Guaranty Page. Most companies have some liability statement on their products that should be included in the catalog. This is a statement from the company's attorney that must be included verbatim. It is unfortunate because a tight warranty statement often provides good sales ammunition that may be lost in formal legal language.

The design of the warranty page should be simple. Do not use gaudy trim or designs to set off the statement; this is an antiquated treatment, often still used, that sells nothing. The power of suggestion is immeasurable. Why suggest that a company is outdated by using an antiquated treatment of the warranty?

Foreword. Most dictionaries define foreword as a "word said beforehand." In catalog application the definition must be stretched to a "statement given beforehand." The catalog foreword should sum up the catalog contents concisely. It differs from the introduction only in the length of the message. The design of the foreword page should be simple and reflect the character of the catalog contents.

Contents. The primary function of the table of contents is to aid the reader in finding a particular point of interest as fast as possible. The contents page reflects the outline or organization of the catalog. If possible, the contents should be one page. If an additional page is required, plan the contents as a two-page spread. There is a danger in having contents pages backing one another; the reader may see only the first page and surmise that the catalog contains only what is seen on the first contents page. With facing pages this does not happen.

The design of the contents must be simple, functional, and most important, legible. Particular attention to spacing, type face, and size is required. Eliminate the obvious; do not use the words "chapter," "section," and "page number" at the heads of columns in the contents. This is understood and is not necessary. Many times, even the page heading "Contents" can be eliminated if the contents cannot be confused with tabular matter in the first few pages of the catalog. Several typical contents pages are shown in Figure 10.

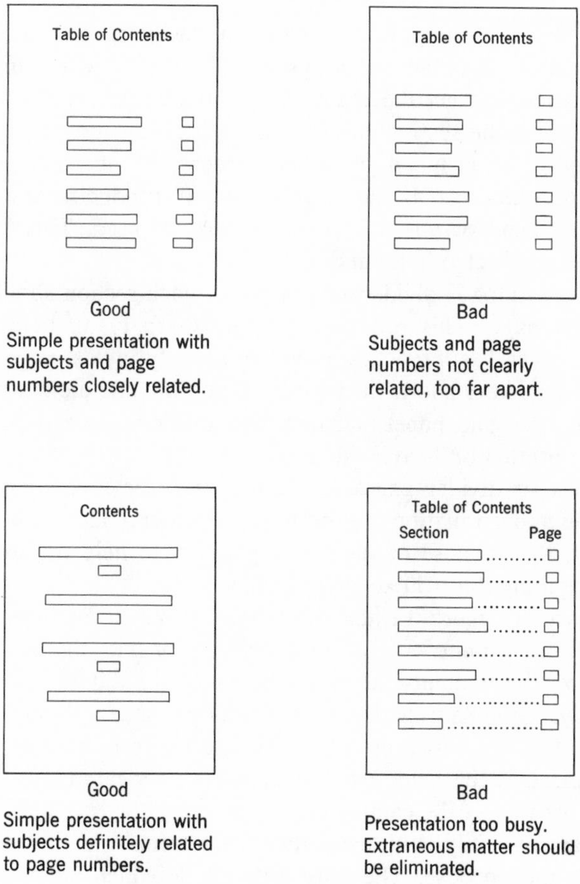

Good

Simple presentation with subjects and page numbers closely related.

Bad

Subjects and page numbers not clearly related, too far apart.

Good

Simple presentation with subjects definitely related to page numbers.

Bad

Presentation too busy. Extraneous matter should be eliminated.

Figure 10.   Typical contents pages.

Introduction. There are no special requirements for the introductory page. This page, however, must be designed so that it fits naturally into the catalog. The same basic format, type face, and so forth should be retained. The introductory page can be used to discuss quantity discounts, minimum billings, or service information, including a list of Sales and Service offices with addresses.

Company Profile. The company profile or history is a page that often contains a letter from the president, the founder's picture, or pictures of many buildings. There are countless catalogs with this type of uninteresting page. New, fresh ideas should be used to project the size of the company and the extent of its products.

Indexing

One of the most important factors in designing a successful catalog is the development of an index system. The index works in conjunction with the contents to get the reader to the right place in the shortest time. The catalog must be sectionalized for an index system to work. All similiar products must be grouped in logical order and, if possible, should be contained on one page. If there are too many products for a single page, a two-page spread or an entire section must be used. This logical breakdown must be reflected in the index.

When the catalog is divided into sections, each section should be headed by an index page. This provides a clear, sharp break between sections. There are several approaches used to identify index pages. The most popular methods are shown in Figure 11 and include die-cut thumb indexing, die-cut tabs, and panel bleeding. The index pages can be a distinctive color or be printed on heavier stock.

The index or divider pages can if necessary be used to give more detailed contents information. Coordinate the index pages with the contents. Remember, the purpose of the index pages is to help the user find items fast; use anything that will accomplish this.

As shown in Figure 12, the cover can serve as an index when there is a minimum number of sections or divisions in the catalog. With a cover index, the contents and breakdown of the catalog become evident immediately. Often a functional or numerical index should be included. These indexes are most useful when specific products are well-known and recognized in the field. Functional and numerical indexes are normally located at the rear of the catalog.

Only careful study and evaluation determine which indexing system best serves the purpose. The only criterion is which index system makes

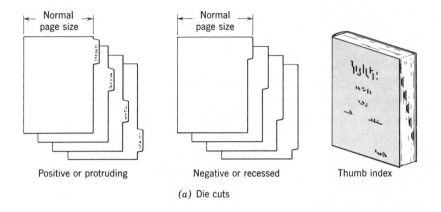

Positive or protruding   Negative or recessed   Thumb index

(*a*) Die cuts

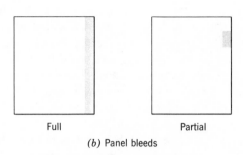

Full   Partial

(*b*) Panel bleeds

Figure 11. Methods of indexing.

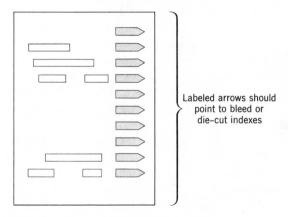

Labeled arrows should point to bleed or die-cut indexes

Figure 12. Typical cover index.

it easier for the catalog user to locate specific items in the catalog. The designer must use any trick to create a working index.

The Body of the Catalog

The decision on page size must be made in conjunction with the decision to use single-, double-, or triple-column text pages and the trim size. Several factors affect this decision. If the catalog body is mainly text, with few illustrations, a single-column narrow page is usually most desirable; however, the double- and triple-column presentations are more flexible if many illustrations, charts, and graphs are used. Another advantage of double- and triple-columns is that the individual columns are not so wide as the single-column text. This factor affects readability and should be considered when the catalog text is lengthy. The selection of type also affects readability. Type selection is discussed in the following chapter.

In the publications field trim size is usually an arbitrary decision based primarily on the use of the publication. The most popular trim size for a catalog is the standard $8\frac{1}{2}'' \times 11''$ page. If a smaller page size is used, the catalog may be hidden by other larger catalogs in the same bookcase. Using the standard trim size usually results in substantial savings in printing and paper costs; many printers offer lower prices for standard trim sizes and majority of modern paper making machines produce paper rolls that are designed to give maximum economy when used in $8\frac{1}{2}'' \times 11''$ publications.

Instead of trying to make rules for such items as trim size, number of columns, margins, and spacing between columns, it is better to study individual pages from existing printed matter that show these factors. Determining them is like choosing paper stock or printing; it is not an isolated choice. All items must be considered, and the best blend of all factors should be used to obtain the best over-all presentation.

To help determine the proper format always consider the two-page spread (facing pages). Opposite pages must be compatible and fit together as a unit. When attempting to visualize a two-page spread, it is often helpful to sketch tentative trim sizes, margins, and number of columns. Include running heads, folios, titles, and other significant format patterns on the sketches.

When basic page specifications are settled, the design process goes into the preliminary proof stage. While the design details are considered one by one, each development must be analyzed against the over-all concept and all alternatives given careful consideration.

To proceed with preliminary design proofing, gather typical information that is to be included in the catalog. Obtain at least one specimen of each material to give the designer an idea of the design problems. This is particularly important for any difficult or dense areas. His design solution must provide a smooth presentation for all catalog matter. Remember, design changes at this stage cost nothing, whereas in later phases they can be extremely expensive. Face and solve difficult design problems as soon as possible.

ILLUSTRATIONS AND CATALOG DESIGN

Illustrations are included in a catalog for two purposes: one is to inform and clarify and the other is to motivate. Without illustrations the text is incomplete and the catalog has no sales impact. Select any catalog and mentally remove the illustrations; this leaves obvious gaps and voids the marketing appeal.

Frequently, illustrations that are considered motivational are included in the catalog to break the monotony of straight textural or tabular manner, to make a specific fact clearer, or to provide emphasis. Except for the cover, none should be included solely for esthetic reasons. Often the selection of motivational illustrations is left to the designer who determines those to be included after he reads the copy.

Whether illustrations are essential (informative) or motivational is not the main point. Any illustration should be used that increases the user's comprehension of the catalog material. While considering the purpose of illustrations, some thought must be given to illustrations that will create the proper tone for the catalog. As previously mentioned, photographs are the most effective. Other illustrations are discussed in Chapter 7.

SYMMETRY AND COLOR IN CATALOG DESIGN

Symmetry is a key word in catalog design. Unusual eye-catching arrangements of illustrations, text, and color should be avoided. This arrangement does not last, and unless catalogs are reissued several times a year it should have a more standard symmetrical design. The eye is most accustomed and most receptive to symmetrical layout. The presentation has greater effect if the user need not follow a nonsymmetrical pattern. Careful use of color can provide (a) separation, (b) emphasis, (c) breakup, and (d) coherence. Remember, additional colors increase costs; use them wisely and get your money's worth.

6

TYPE SELECTION

One of the most controversial design subjects is the choice of type for text and display lines. The design of type faces is involved with tradition and many typographers rebel against designs that depart from tradition. An important function of the designer is the selection of a tasteful type face that reconciles esthetic qualities with practical limitations. A majority of catalog readers are unaware of vaious type faces. Do not assume, however, that they will not respond to good typography.

STANDARD MEASUREMENTS

Typographers have standard measurements that are universally adopted in the industry. The two most important units are the *pica* and the *point*.

The Pica

The pica unit is used for linear measurements of type, illustration, gutter, or margin areas. The line length as well as the copy depths are normally specified in picas; for example, a block of copy might be specified to be set 15 picas wide and 30 picas deep. The practical relationship of the pica to the point and the inch are as follows:

- $\frac{1}{12}$ pica = 1 point = $\frac{1}{72}$ inch
- $\frac{1}{2}$ pica = 6 points = $\frac{1}{12}$ inch
- 1 pica = 12 points = $\frac{1}{6}$ inch
- 6 picas = 72 points = 1 inch

The Point

The point measures 0.013837 inch or nearly $\frac{1}{72}$ of an inch. All hot-metal type, whether foundry or machine composition, is designated in points (10 point Futura, 12 point Garamond, 8 point Caledonia). Type measurements, particularly the sizes used for catalog work, are generally made from the top of ascenders (such as the letter "b") to the bottom of descenders (such as the letter "g"). Technically, this is not correct. As shown in Figure 13, the body of the type is the actual type measurement. The difference is usually negligible.

Type is graduated from 3 to 144 points in size, although in catalog work there is little need for anything more than 48 points. Figure 14 shows a typical graduated scale of type sizes. There are many exceptions. Many typographers have type available between the sizes shown, especially around 9 and 11 point sizes. Typographers often furnish a book, chart, or cards to show the specimens available. This information is compiled

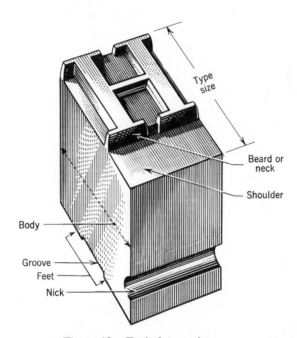

Figure 13. Typical type size.

Figure 14. Type-size graduation scales.

quite carefully. In most instances it includes both upper- and lower-case characters in various sizes and in large enough blocks to give the designer a clear picture to help his visualization process. The use of these informative aids is discussed later in this chapter under the headings of character counting and copy fitting.

Close observation of several type faces in the same point size reveals slightly different character heights. Letters of some faces are more extended in width whereas others are condensed. These are the factors that give character and style to the different type faces.

The point unit of measurement is also applied to word and letterspacing. Letterspacing can be used effectively to provide emphasis. The sudden change in contrast becomes a key factor in providing this emphasis. Any copy becomes conspicuous if it is spaced differently from surrounding copy. Figure 15 shows several examples of the effect spacing has on presentation. It is important that the designer be tasteful when using word and letterspacing because it affects the over-all presentation.

The common word and letterspaces are hair spaces ($\frac{1}{2}$ or 1 point), thin spaces ($\frac{1}{16}$ to $\frac{1}{4}$ em), normal spaces ($\frac{1}{3}$ em), en ($\frac{1}{2}$ em), em, 2 em and so forth. The em is an important unit to typographers. It is a square of the type size; for example, an em of 10-point type measures 10 points wide and 10 points high and of 8-point type, 8 points square. The em is considered a unit measurement, the quantity of type. If a line of type 4 inches long (288 points is set in 10-point type, the line

Letterspacing can be used to provide emphasis.

Line set with 1-point spacing

Letterspacing can be used to provide emphasis.

Line set with 3-point spacing

Letterspacing can be used to provide emphasis.

Line set with 6-point spacing

Letterspacing can be used to provide emphasis.

Line set with 8-point spacing

Figure 15.   Examples of word and letterspacing.

is said to contain 28.8 ems (288 ÷ 10 = 28.8). Many typographers estimate costs using the em-count as a basis.

Another major consideration in specifying type is the spacing between lines, commonly referred to as *leading*. In addition to type size and word and letterspacing, the over-all copy depends on the selection of leading. Neither the length of line nor the size of type should be selected without proper consideration to leading. Generally, larger type faces require more leading to avoid confusion and increase readability. Longer lines require more leading to distinguish them and help the reader go from the end of one line to the beginning of the next. Another consideration is the style of type face used; faces with short ascenders and descenders should have more leading than those with long ascenders and descenders.

The terms most used in specifying leading are solid, 1-point leaded, 2-point leaded, and so forth. Several examples of different leading are shown in Figure 16.

The designer depends on his judgment when determining leading. Up to a point increased leading means improved readability. With so many

> Neither the length of line nor the type size should be selected without proper consideration to leading.

Copy set solid

> Neither the length of line nor the type size should be selected without proper consideration to leading.

Copy set 1-point leaded

> Neither the length of line nor the type size should be selected without proper consideration to leading.

Copy set 2-point leaded

> Neither the length of line nor the type size should be selected without proper consideration to leading.

Copy set 3-point leaded

Figure 16. Examples of leading.

variables, the choice of leading becomes a matter of visualization. Generally, body copy should not be leaded more than one-third its type-face size.

METHODS OF SETTING TYPE

There are three basic methods of setting type—monotype, linotype, and photocomposition. Each has its advantages and disadvantages and are discussed below.

Monotype Machines

Monotype means what the name implies; one letter or character is set at a time. An advantage of monotype is that it is easier to make corrections. Other advantages include large type selection, easier setting of mathematical formulas, and easier setting of tabular material. The main disadvantage of monotype is that generally it is more expensive than linotype. If present-day improvements continue, this factor may shortly be eliminated.

The monotype process requires two machines, keyboard and casting equipment. An operator types out copy on a keyboard that resembles a typewriter and produces a perforated tape. Each character or letter is represented by a different code of perforations. The perforated tape is then run through the casting machine which molds each character or letter individually. Casts for individual letters are contained in a matrix case that normally holds up to 255 characters. Because characters are individually casted, they must be handled with care.

Linotype Machines

Although the monotype machine sets one character or letter at a time, the linotype machine sets an entire line of type to the desired width. The advantages of a linotype are (a) it is cheaper, (b) it is faster, and (c) the type is easier to store. The disadvantages are that a smaller selection of type than monotype is available and it is more difficult to set tabular matter and mathematical formulas.

In the linotype process an operator types out copy on a typewriter-like keyboard. A magazine that contains 180 types of character and letter is selected and inserted into the machine. As the keyboard is punched, a related character mat will be released from the magazine and placed into an assembler. As a line is filled or completed with character mats, molten metal pours into the assembler and casts a complete line. The molded line is ejected and the individual character mats are returned to the magazine for future use.

Photocomposition Machines

Photocomposition machines cannot be classified as hot-metal machines, although they produce copy that resembles the product of hot-metal composition. The field of photocomposition has made large advancements in recent years to provide a faster, lower-cost method of providing type. Because of its late start, not nearly as many type faces are available as with hot-metal methods, although many of the more popular faces are available.

Basically, the photocomposition machine consists of a light-projection system, character matrix, shutters, optical system, film holder, and developer. The optical system provides a means of enlargement or reduction while using one set of character matrix; the versatility of quick size changes is a major advantage with this system. Depending on the photocomposition machine, the end product is either a negative or positive proof.

It is not intended to recommend the use of one machine over another, only to make you aware of each. When the catalog program reaches the stage when type must be bought, obtain quotations from typographers using different methods and choose accordingly. Modern typesetting machinery produces excellent results no matter which method is selected.

TYPE FACES

Space allotment makes it impossible to examine and explain all the type faces that might be used in a catalog. In fact, it would be unfair to specify individual type faces that should be used. The choice of type faces must be appropriate to the catalog being prepared. The choice is somewhat personal. Designers should select type for some definite reasons. Type can give not only readability but tone; for example, some faces appear bold while others appear unassuming, decorative, plain, formal, or social.

Choosing the type face for display heads must be closely related to the selection of body type. Display heads include headings, subheadings, chapter titles, section titles, product names, or categories. The choice must be harmonious. Again this is a matter of taste and judgment.

Generally, the faces used for catalog preparation should have a pleasing character. Some of the most widely used include Century, Baskerville, Bodoni, Garamond, Venus, Caledonia, and Caslon. Any of these or similar faces have a high degree of legibility and readability and are particularly suitable for large blocks of copy, Sans-serif type faces, such as Futura and News Gothic, are also used but are considered harder to read when large blocks of copy are set.

COPY FITTING

Copy fitting is the process of determining final type sizes, measures, and areas from manuscript copy. Before copy can be typeset, it is necessary to calculate the area the typeset copy will occupy. This is particularly true if the copy is tight.

There are two steps required to copy fit accurately: (a) the manuscript copy must be carefully measured, and (b) the measurement must be applied to the selected type face and size.

The measurement of manuscript copy is performed by a character count. This consists of counting the characters, letters, and spaces in the copy, on a paragraph basis, usually by measuring lines or areas. There are various methods for measuring typewritten manuscript copy. The most convenient is to use a pica (12 point) or elite (10 point) typewriter when typing the manuscript. Because each typewriter character occupies the same space, the exact number of characters in each line can be measured with a ruler. The average character count for a line can then be multiplied by the number of lines in the paragraph to determine the total character count. This count can now be applied against the character-count table given for each type face in the specimen books. Remember, leading does not affect the number of lines but does affect the depth of the typeset copy.

To demonstrate copy fitting more clearly assume a layout that requires copy to be 24 picas wide. The selected type face and size is 10 point Bodoni Bold. The character-count table indicates that 10 point Bodoni Bold has 2.8 characters per pica. Multiplying 24 picas by 2.8 equals 67.2 type characters. This means that each line of typeset copy is allowed 67.2 characters. Divide 67.2 into the total number of characters counted in your manuscript copy. This results in the total of solid set lines in your final copy. To calculate copy depth multiply the number of lines by the leading and add this to the total of the type size times the number of lines. When space is at a premium, the character count should be made as precisely as possible.

All competent typographers have copy-fitting tables or aids for determining character counts. Often, this operation will be performed by them, if desired.

PREPARING COPY FOR TYPOGRAPHERS

Clear, legible manuscript copy is the most important item to the typographer. The manuscript should be accompanied by rough layouts and proper type specifications.

Making rough layouts for the typographer is a key function of the designer. Usually, good layouts are a result of trial and error, work and rework until the best presentation is obtained. Rough layouts can be made on sketch pads or preprinted forms that have standard format markings. All areas must be clearly identified, including page folios, with page dimensions. A rough layout should be made of every page in the catalog. Doing

MARK	EXPLANATION	EXAMPLE	MARK	EXPLANATION	EXAMPLE
ℓ	Take out character indicated.	ℓ The proof.	¶	Start paragraph.	¶ read. The
∧	Left out, insert.	ℎ Te proof.	no ¶	No paragraph; run in.	no ¶ marked. The proof.
#	Insert space.	# Theproof.	⌐	Raise.	⌐ The proof
9	Turn inverted letter.	9 The proof.	⌐⌐	Lower.	The proof.
x	Broken letter.	x The proof.	⊏	Move left.	⊏ The proof.
⊥	Push down space.	⊥ The proof.	⊐	Move right.	⊐ The proof.
eq#	Even space.	eq# A good proof.	‖	Align type.	‖ Three men. Two women.
⌣	Less space.	The proof.	=	Straighten line.	= The proof.
⌒	Close up; no space.	⌒ The proof.	⊙	Insert period.	⊙ The proof.
tr.	Transpose.	tr A proof good.	,/	Insert comma.	,/ The proof.
wf	Wrong font.	wf The proof.	:/	Insert colon.	:/ The proof.
lc	Lower case.	lc The Proof.	;/	Insert semicolon.	;/ The proof.
sc	Small capitals.	The proof. sc (The) proof.	V	Insert apostrophe.	V The boys proof.
c+sc	Capitals and small capitals.	The proof. c+sc The proof.	VV	Insert quotation marks.	VV Marked it proof.
caps	Capitals.	The proof. caps (The) proof.	=/	Insert hyphen.	=/ A proofmark.
				Insert inferior figure.	Water, H₂O
P	Capitalize.	P The proof.		Insert superior figure.	A² + B² = C
ital	Italic.	The proof. ital The proof.	/	Insert exclamation mark.	/ Prove it
rom	Roman.	rom The (proof.)	?	Insert question mark.	? Is it good
			P	Query for author.	P was The proof read by
bf	Bold face.	The proof. bf (The) proof.	[/]	Insert brackets.	[/] The Jones boy ...
			(/)	Insert parentheses.	(/) The proof 1
stet	Let it stand.	The proof. stet The proof.	/≠/	Insert 1-en dash.	/≠/ The proof
			/⊥/	Insert 1-em dash.	/⊥/ The proof
out sc	Out, see copy.	out sc He proof.	/≥/	Insert 2-em dash.	/≥/ The proof
spell out	Spell out.	spell out King (Geo.)	□	Indent 1 em.	□ The proof.
			⊞	Indent 2 ems.	⊞ The proof.
			⊟	Indent 3 ems.	⊟ The proof.

Figure 17.   Standard proofreader's marks.

this eliminates problems that may result when copy does not fit. Pay particular attention to tight-fitting pages, Recheck all figures.

The typographer uses a language that is clear and concise. This language is in the form of standard proofreader's marks that are given in Figure 17. The margin of the manuscript should include indications of size, name of type face, spacing, leading, line lengths, and centered or flush instructions. Keep all instructions specific and adjacent to the manuscript copy to which they pertain. If a comprehensive layout accompanies the copy, many times only the type name and size need be marked. For best results review marked-up manuscript with the typographer. Many times he will have helpful hints that will improve your catalog. Visit and tour his shop. Learn as much as possible about his operation; this places you in a better position to get what you want.

GALLEY PROOFS

The next step in the catalog program is the receipt of galley proofs from the typographer. A galley proof is pulled on a galley or proof press. The purpose of galley proof is to enable the writer and designer to check for typographic errors and to make minor corrections in copy, centering, and spacing. The galley proofs need not be of high quality but must be legible. The designer at this time can decide if he wants the typographer to furnish reproducible galley proofs or page proofs. If there are large amounts of copy, the typographer can save designer time by making up the final reproducible page; however, if the layout is complex or there are many tables, graphs, and illustrations, the designer may decide to buy reproducible galleys and do the final page makeup himself. Consult the typographer and get his estimate for producing final pages; it might be more economical.

All galley proofs must be proofread carefully against the manuscript. Although most typographers proofread their material, there is too much at stake to risk possible errors, no matter who is at fault. All corrections should be made in the typographer's language. (See Figure 17.)

CAMERA-READY REPRODUCIBLES

The typographer, upon receipt of the annotated galley proofs, proceeds to make all necessary corrections. After the corrections are made, he produces reproducible proofs either in galleys or complete pages or he can supply the actual metal if letterpress printing is used. The type must be locked up tightly so that all copy is square and placed on a repro press to produce reproducible proofs. The repro press is capable of doing a first-class printing job; in fact, it is generally a miniature of the press on which the final catalogs will be printed. The quality of the reproducible copy has a direct bearing on the quality of the final, printed catalog. Poor quality, such as uneven lines and broken or filled-in letters, should be rejected.

Reproducible proofs are usually produced on coated paper, either glossy or dull. The coated paper can also have a pressure-sensitive adhesive backing which makes it more convenient to prepare page mechanicals. (Mechanical preparation is discussed in Chapter 7.)

Reproducible proofs can also be supplied on acetate or transparent plastic sheets which are helpful when using multiplecolored layouts. These sheets are also available with pressure-sensitive adhesive backing.

Remember, reproducible proofs should provide as perfect an image as possible. Perfection is impossible to obtain, but strive to obtain the closest degree possible. Settle for nothing but the best.

7

ILLUSTRATIONS

In the preceding chapters illustrations referred to ideas or rough sketches. These ideas and sketches must be developed into final illustrations for use in the catalog. This task should be performed by professional artists who are skilled in the techniques of graphical expression. The purpose of this chapter is to explain the activities necessary to produce good, final illustrations that are compatible with printing specifications.

In addition to artistic functions such as drawing, inking, airbrushing, and photographing, there are mechanics that also must be performed. Among these are mounting, using register marks, determining the most effective screens, and sizing illustrations. None of these mechanical operations is difficult, but they all are important if the best results are to be obtained.

The larger the catalog, the more important it is to organize the production of final illustrations. All illustrations should be assigned a key number. This eliminates confusion later when the artwork and copy are being combined to form the final page mechanical. The key number should be repeated in its proper space on the text repro.

Line artwork for a catalog should be drawn at least twice its final size. There are two reasons for doing this: (a) most illustrations that are the size they are to appear in the catalog are too small for an artist to work with and (b) illustrations that are reduced will reproduce more sharply. Lines that may be somewhat frayed in the enlarged artwork blend and create clear, sharp lines in the reduced version. The opposite is true if artwork is enlarged, all defects are magnified and the results are often disappointing. To obtain proper line weights in the reduced illustration, the line weights must be made heavier in the enlarged original. The degree of line weight is a factor in the scaled reduction.

There are two categories of illustrations that are used in a catalog, informative and representative. Informative illustrations are used to depict specific facts, such as outline drawings and wiring diagrams. Representative illustrations are almost always photographs and are essential to an effective catalog.

DIFFERENT TYPES OF ILLUSTRATION

The types of illustration are related directly to the types of camera copy. The camera distinguishes between line and continuous-tone subjects. Line copy is shot with maximum contrast, thus producing every line as solid black and all background as white. The essential requirements for good line copy are sharpness and contrast or, stated simply, good blacks and whites. Anything short of this might compromise the result and provide additional work for the printer's cameraman.

Continuous-tone copy can never be printed exactly as the original copy; theoretically, printers can come fairly close. The important point is that some degradation takes place between the original and the reproduction. Good printed results are completely dependent on the quality of the original artwork. Usually, photographs are the only continuous-tone artwork used in the catalog.

GUIDE LINES FOR GOOD PHOTOGRAPHY

The importance of good photographs in a catalog cannot be emphasized enough. When photographs are required, they should be taken by a competent professional photographer. Preparation of halftone artwork (photographs) is a delicate business, but with good photography and careful planning it can be provided at reasonable cost. Almost any photograph can be salvaged for catalog use if it is heavily airbrushed. Airbrushing services are expensive, and although they are often required some efforts should be made to keep airbrushing at a minimum. A little time spent in planning to obtain a clean, sharp, contrasting print is repaid by reduction of the amount of airbrush retouching required.

The equipment or products to be photographed should be clean (when possible) and should be positioned to show all interesting items. One never knows what may interest a potential buyer; therefore the more that is shown the better. The subject should be well-lighted to eliminate undesirable heavy, harsh shadows and the camera positioned to eliminate unwanted distortions. Generally, photographs are most effective when taken with the camera positioned approximately where the viewer's eye would be when looking at the subject. This adds a sense of reality to the picture.

For domestic-product catalogs the approach to photography changes. The human interest quality may mean the difference between a highly effective presentation and another dull one. The projection of the human factor is vital to create a good public image. Generally, the human-interest factor cannot be defined; it is there or it is not. If products are used in the domestic market, use a qualified commercial photographer.

PREPARING PHOTOGRAPHS FOR THE CATALOG

Once the photograph has been taken, it must be processed properly for reproduction. The first consideration is the kind of print required. There are three basic prints available: (a) glossy, (b) semimatte, and (c) matte. Most printers prefer that halftone artwork be prepared with glossy prints. Glossy prints are sharper and have more contrast, but new methods make it possible to use semimatte or matte prints.

Semimatte and matte prints are more durable than glossy prints. Glossy prints have a tendency to pick up fingerprints and scratches and the emulsion is subject to cracking. Probably the biggest restriction of the glossy print is the retouching process. Often glossy prints are curled and must be dampened, flattened, and carefully mounted. Extreme care must be taken when removing friskets or the emulsion will come off. The glossy surface will accept only airbrushing or spotting, thus limiting the retoucher to these techniques. With a matte finish the retoucher can use pencils, stamps, chalks, and erasers in addition to airbrushing and spotting. Many cameramen automatically tone down the glossy surface by using a dulling spray on glossy prints. Ask your printer for his recommendations before deciding to use glossy, semimatte, or matte prints.

After receiving prints from the photographer, the artist must decide whether retouching is necessary. Often, retouching is the only way to obtain an acceptable illustration. Although retouching is expensive, it should be used when necessary. The importance of the catalog certainly justifies it.

All photographs, whether they are to be retouched or not, should be mounted on standard illustration board. Mounting is a simple procedure. It consists of applying rubber cement to the back of the print and to the illustration board, allowing the cement to dry partially, and placing the print on the board, while carefully burnishing the print flat. Using a rigid mount such as standard illustration board makes it easy to obtain a satisfactory bond that is free of air bubbles.

If background clutter must be removed from the mounted print, it can be trimmed off carefully by cutting around the desired image and lifting off the part of the print that contains the background clutter. Another method is to apply carefully white retouching paint around the outside edges of the desired image. Most white retouching paints do not dry out and are fluid enough to be applied with a ruling pen. They must adhere to glossy surfaces if glossy prints are used for halftone illustrations. Mounting and background elimination procedures do not require much experience and often can be performed by less-talented illustrators. This promotes efficiency and frees more experienced illustrators for more difficult catalog assignments.

If index numbers or other lettering must be added to final printed illustrations, a clear acetate overlay is added to the mounted photograph. All numbers and lettering are then applied directly to the overlay. Always include several registration marks both on the mounted artwork and the overlay. Using this method requires the printer to take two shots, one screened shot of the photograph and one line shot of the overlay. This two-shot method produces a clear reproduction of the halftone area and solid black reproduction of the indexing material.

Indexing material can be applied directly to the photograph, if desired. The printer will screen both the photographic print and lettering. A slight screen pattern will also be evident in the background. This can be dropped out by the printer, but this will increase the printing cost.

LINE ARTWORK

All line artwork must be designed so that it depicts exactly what is intended in the simplest form. The size of line artwork is based entirely on its function. If many details are included, a large illustration is necessary; on the contrary, a simple drawing with little or no lettering can be much smaller and still perform its job.

The shape of the drawing is often a factor that is either lightly considered or not considered at all. The drawing shape is largely an esthetic matter, but the important factor is that the content not be sacrificed. An effort should be made to make interesting and varied shapes. Page after page with similar rectangular-shaped drawings can become dull.

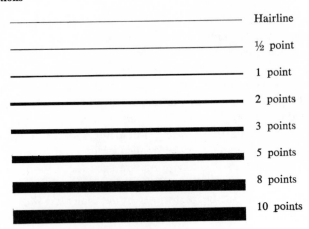

Hairline

½ point

1 point

2 points

3 points

5 points

8 points

10 points

Figure 18.   Various line weights.

When selecting line weights and lettering size, the planned reduction of the artwork must be considered. Reduced letter sizes should never be smaller than 6 points, with 10 points the more preferred size. Various line weights are shown in Figure 18. There is no general rule that applies to line weights in final illustrations. Do not make them too heavy; use common sense. It is desirable to have lines that form the outer extremities of the drawing slightly heavier than all others. This helps to tie the illustration together.

Line drawings can be prepared on linen or illustration board. Good results are obtained from either method. There are no particular advantages of one over the other. The main difference is that board artwork can be stored flat, whereas linen artwork can be rolled. If artwork storage is a factor, make your selection accordingly.

SIZING ILLUSTRATIONS

Illustration sizing or scaling is a simple matter once it is understood. The principle of sizing is based on the geometric axiom that all rectangles of the same proportions have the same diagonal. Without getting more involved in mathematical terms, it is sufficient to state that many proportional devices that perform the necessary scaling calculations are available. Several of the more popular instruments are the proportional dial, the proportional wheel, and the proportional scale shown in Figure 19. Using

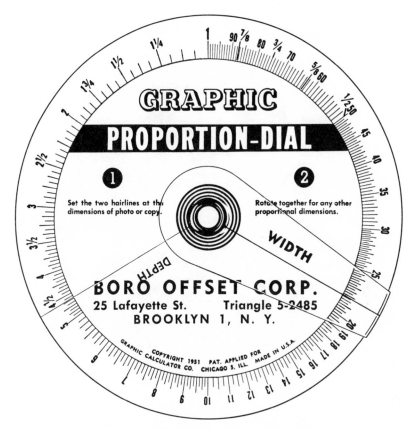

Figure 19. Proportional scaling device (dial).
Courtesy of Graphic Calculator Company, Barrington, Illinois.

any of these devices reduces calculations to a simple mechanical process. Set one pair of desired dimensions and all other readings are given in the same proportion.

PREPARING MULTICOLORED ILLUSTRATIONS

The preparation of multicolored illustrations should be coordinated with the printer. As explained previously, some form of color separation is necessary to print multicolored illustrations. For photographs the separation is by process color. If the colors can be separated mechanically by the illustrator, printing costs will be less. To provide mechanical color separation the illustrator builds an illustration mechanical. This process

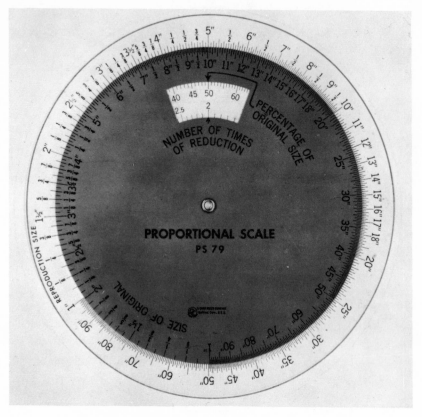

Figure 19 (continued).   Proportional scaling device (wheel).

is shown in Figure 20. The basic black portions of the illustration is prepared on the illustration board; then a clear acetate overlay is added for each color. Each overlay must have precise registration marks, for poor registration provides unacceptable reproductions. If color areas do not touch or cross over one another, they can be combined on one overlay. If this is done, be sure to supply detailed instructions to the printer. The extra work required to provide additional colors in a catalog should not inhibit their use. Remember, a catalog is a field showroom.

If process-color printing is used, the best possible colored artwork must be supplied. In all printing processes a slight degradation occurs in reproduction. Because additional lenses are required in process-color printing, the increased degradation makes it even more important to have high-quality copy. Process-color printing is discussed in Chapter 8.

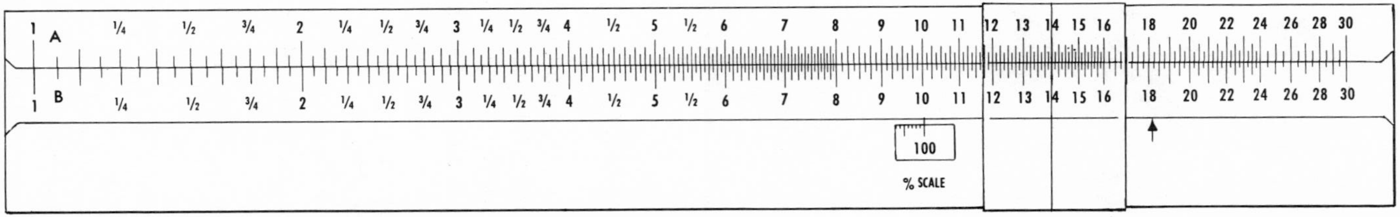

Figure 19 (continued). Proportional scaling device (scale).

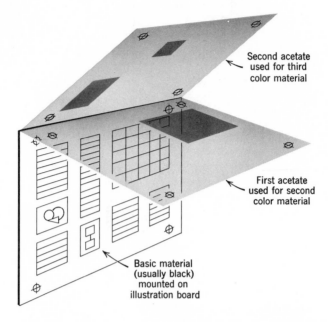

Second acetate
used for third
color material

First acetate
used for second
color material

Basic material
(usually black)
mounted on
illustration board

Figure 20.   Building a multicolored illustration mechanical.

PREPARING PAGE MECHANICALS

Preparing page mechanicals is a key function of the illustration group. The page mechanical used for offset lithography is camera copy, consisting of all page elements, which is marked for maximum economy in platemaking. Platemaking economy is obtained when minimum camera work is required; the target is to shoot a page with one exposure. To do this, each page element (text or artwork) must be in the same scale and all page elements must be in proper position.

A separate consideration must be made for halftone illustrations. There are two methods available for handling halftones. In the first, which is now the more popular, the page elements, excluding the halftone illustration, are shot to produce a line negative. The halftone illustration is then shot to produce a properly sized screened negative. The screened negative is then stripped into the line negative in its allocated position to produce a composite negative.

The second method of handling halftone illustrations is to produce suitably-reduced, screened, positive stats. The screened stats are then pasted into their allocated positions on the page mechanicals and a line negative made of the composite page mechanical. This method is gaining popularity for the development of finer lenses are producing top-quality stats. This is the key to the successful use of this method. Another advantage is that all page elements are positioned exactly where you want them; there is no margin for the printer to strip a negative into the wrong area. Call your printer and question him about both methods. The majority of printers probably still prefer the first method, although the second can result in saving printing costs with little quality lost in reproduction.

When preparing mechanicals for multicolor printing, the same method is used as in the preparation of multicolored illustration mechanicals (see Figure 20). For each color an individual acetate overlay is developed. This keeps instructions to the printer simple and results in a more economical printing price.

The paste-up of mechanicals can be performed in many ways. Rubber cement, tape, wax, or pressure-sensitive, adhesive-backed paper are the most popular means. Wax coaters that speed up mechanical preparation are available. The page elements are passed through rollers that apply a thin coat of adhesive wax on the underside of the sheet. The copy can then be placed in position on the page mechanical. The advantage of the waxing is that the material can be lifted and shifted more easily than with other paste-up methods. It also eliminates the glue pots, and it is easier to clean the copy after paste-up is completed. Always clean mechanicals thoroughly before submitting them to a printer. Remember paper edges, smears, dirt, cement excess, and cuts all will be picked up by the printer's camera. This increases his camera work and, as always, increases his costs. All page mechanicals should be flapped. This simple operation takes only a short time and provides good protection to valuable page mechanicals.

Copies of page mechanicals can now be made and submitted to the designated authorities before printing. Do not print without this authorization. Before releasing the page mechanicals, there is one more extremely important item that must be prepared—ample printing instructions. Instructions must be clear and complete. Call in the printer and have a conference. Something that may seem clear to you may not be to a cameraman; they have their own language. Check the mechanicals for register marks, indication of bleeds, screen size, trim size, dimensions, scale, cropmarks, and color scheme.

Many cameramen use the relative percentage for reducing or enlarging copy. This has always been a point of confusion, and it is safer to indicate the exact final size desired. The cameramen have proportional scales and can do their own figuring. The information supplied to them is clear and, therefore, the printed results should be exactly those requested. Use carefully placed cropmarks to eliminate confusion absolutely. Instructions should be written directly on the protective flap. Do not bear down hard when writing for an impression may be made on the reproducible copy that the camera might pick up.

In summary, keep in close contact with your printer at all times. Good printer coordination is beneficial throughout the program and provides over-all printing economy.

8

PRINTING

Printing costs are one of the more significant factors in a catalog program. When selecting a printer, it is most important that the printing job fit the printer's equipment. Competent printers are not likely to put a job on an unsuitable press, but it is best to know some guidelines to avoid this costly mistake. This chapter gives some basic knowledge of the various printing processes and the presses on which these processes are performed.

PRINTING PROCESSES

There are three basic printing processes that are used for catalog printing—letterpress, offset lithography, and gravure. Letterpress is a term that applies to printing methods that depend on raised images or surfaces, as opposed to the flat or plain surfaces used in offset lithography and gravure. As shown in Figure 21, the letterpress plate has raised surfaces on which ink is applied. The ink is then transferred by placing paper over the inked plate and applying even pressure to the paper. The printing surfaces of offset-lithography plates, on the other hand, are on the plate surface. The plates are specially treated so the printing surfaces will accept greasy ink and repel water. The nonprinting areas have exactly opposite characteristics; they repel the inks and accept the water. The ink is then transferred to paper by placing the paper over the inked plate and applying even pressure to the paper.

As shown in Figure 21, gravure is the opposite of letterpress in many respects. Instead of the printing image being raised above the surface of the plate, it is etched into the plate. Ink is then applied to the plate and a doctor is used to clear the plate surface of excess ink; all etched surfaces are filled with ink. The ink is then transferred to paper through pressure and suction. The various presses used to implement these printing processes are discussed separately.

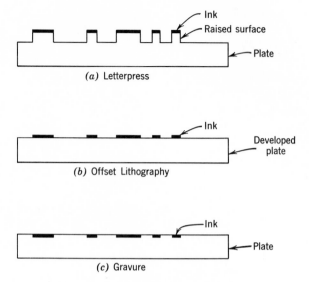

Figure 21.   Basic printing processes.

LETTERPRESS

Letterpress is probably the oldest method of printing and has remained relatively unchanged for years. The recent challenge of offset lithography has necessitated the development of photomechanical platemaking so that letterpress can remain competitive. There are three basic presses used to perform letterpress printing: (a) platen press, (b) flat-bed cylinder press, and (c) rotary press.

The Platen Press

The principle of the platen press is given in Figure 22. In the illustration the clamshell-type platen press is used. In Step *a* the plate is inked and paper is inserted. In Step *b* the clamshell closes the paper against the inked plate after the ink rolls have cleared. Pressure is applied so that ink transfer from plate to paper takes place. In Step *c* the clamshell opens, the paper is ejected, the plate is reinked, and another blank sheet is placed in the press. A second type of platen press, called the sliding or universal platen, is also used. The basic principles are the same; the differences are unimportant for this discussion. The platen press has the ability to control the amount of pressure that is applied in ink transfer. This makes the platen press extremely versatile when using materials other

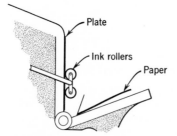

(a) Inking and paper feed

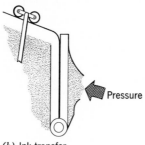

(b) Ink transfer

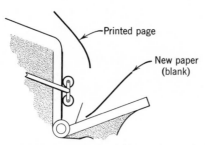

(c) Printed paper ejection, inking, and paper feed

Figure 22.   Principles of the platen press.

than paper on which to print; for example, tissue, cardboard, and plastic materials can all be run on a platen press. Almost any letterpress plate (type, engravings, wood cuts, rubber plates, and electrotypes) can be used. The platen press prints everything from the simplest form to fine-register, multicolor work. The presses are available in many sizes, and the larger and stronger ones can be used in stamping, die-cutting, embossing, and creasing.

The Cylinder Press

The principles of the cylinder press are given in Figure 23. In Step *a* the letterpress plate is being inked and paper is attached to the impression cylinder by grippers. In Step *b* the ink rollers are clearing and the impression roller with the paper is rolled over the inked plate and ink transfer takes place. Step *c* shows the printed sheet being ejected, a new sheet being attached to the impression cylinder, and the plate being reinked for the next cycle. On all cylinder presses, the plate is locked on a flat bed and the impression is made with a revolution of the impression cylinder. A second revolution of the impression cylinder is required to clear the printed sheet; therefore two revolutions of the impression cylinder are necessary to complete one cycle. There are multicolor cylinder presses available; each color requires the basic system shown in Figure 23. A sheet-transfer system is required to transport the sheets from one ink system to the next. There is also a perfecting flat-bed, cylinder press that prints on both sides of the paper during one run through the press.

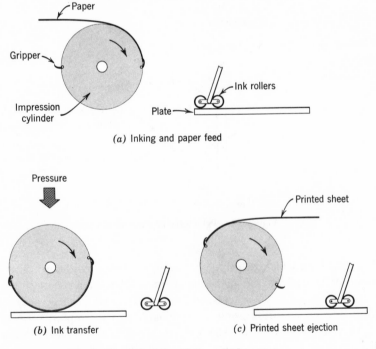

Figure 23. Principles of the cylinder press.

The basic principles of the cylinder press shown in Figure 23 still apply, but a sheet-transfer system is employed that turns the sheet over while transporting it from the first impression cylinder to the second.

The cylinder press accepts most letterpress plates (type, engravings, wood cuts, rubber plates, and electrotypes).

The Rotary Press

The rotary press differs from the cylinder press in that a printing impression is made with every revolution of the impression cylinder rather than with every other revolution. This immediately suggests one of the main advantages of the rotary press; that is, its production rate is higher. The principles of the rotary press are given in Figure 24. The printing plate is curved and clamped to a plate cylinder which revolves against an impression cylinder on one side and ink rollers on the other. Paper is passed between the plate and impression cylinder and ink transfer takes place. The paper may be fed in precut sheets or from a roll; this is the basic distinction among the various rotary presses. A rotary press equipped for printing precut sheets is called a sheet-fed rotary press, whereas a rotary press using paper rolls is called a web-fed rotary press.

In multicolored rotary presses there are two systems used to provide additional colors: (a) the unit system and (b) the common impression system. In the unit system each color has its own impression cylinder and plate cylinder as shown in Figure 24. Thus the number of colors that can be printed during one run through the press is determined by the number of units on the press. Presses are available with up to six units; therefore on such a press, six colors could be printed during one run.

The common impression system has, as its name implies, a common impression cylinder. The principle of this system is illustrated in Figure

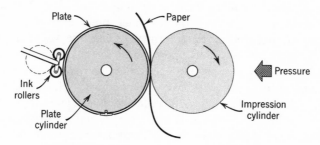

Figure 24. Principles of the rotary press.

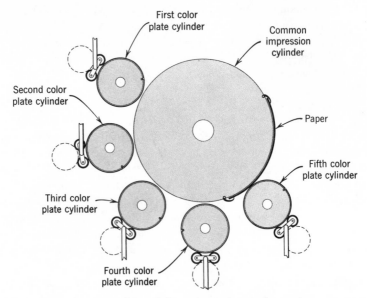

Figure 25.   Principles of the common impression system.

25. Normally, up to five colors can be printed during one run through the press. The quick succession of ink transfer that occurs in this system requires accurate ink control and special quick-dry inks.

The development of the five- and six-color presses makes it possible to get economical, high-quality, multicolored ink for catalog printing. Rotary presses can be equipped with perfecting units, as discussed previously, which provides printing on both sides of the paper during one run through the press.

The high-speed, web-perfecting rotary press provides the ultimate for high-production, good-quality printing. It should be stressed that large runs are necessary to make web-fed printing economical. The set-up time on this press is longer than on all other presses. During set-up time, of course, no material is being printed. Once the web-fed presses are set up, however, their speed compensates for the longer set-up time if the printing run exceeds 50,000 copies. It is dangerous to establish a cutoff point, such as the 50,000 copies mentioned. Modern improvements and innovations are continuously reducing this figure. If a catalog run is at or near 50,000 copies, it is advisable to obtain estimates using both the sheet-fed and web-fed processes. There are many factors that complicate the pricing structure of printing; the best price is obtained when the right press is matched to the job. Competent printers will assist in obtaining this match.

The printing plates used on standard rotary presses can be any plate that can be curved to the plate cylinder's circumference and has the stability and rigidity necessary for high speeds.

A more recent development in letterpress rotary presses is the "wrap-around" rotary. This method preserves most of the advantages of printing from a relief surface at higher speeds and with lower set-up and plate costs. The wrap-around press uses thin, metallic or plastic, shallow-relief plates that can be easily fastened around the plate cylinder. These presses attain speeds of up to 7000 impressions per hour. A continuous development program is in progress in the platemaking area.

OFFSET LITHOGRAPHY

The origin of the term offset lithography describes the principles of this printing method. Lithography is defined as the art of putting writing or designs on stone with a greasy substance and producing printed impressions from them. Basically the smooth, flat-surfaced stone was made into grease-receptive and water-receptive areas. The stone was then dampened with water so that the water-receptive areas would repel the greasy ink that was applied next. After both water and grease were spread, paper was placed carefully over the stone and pressure was applied. This transferred the ink on the stone to the paper. The important distinction is that both the inks and water were on the surface of the stone (plate). Remember, in letterpress printing the surface to be inked is raised, whereas the surface that repels the ink is in relief.

Although stone processing for lithography is still in use today, the development of grained metallic plates (particularly zinc and aluminum) have made lithography a practical method of commercial printing. The metallic plates can be applied easily to the cylinders of rotary presses, a fact that makes possible the fast offset presses on which most lithography is produced today. The processes and activities necessary to prepare material for offset lithography are emphasized because this printing method is presently the most popular for catalog production.

The word "offset" is commonly used when reference is made to offset lithography. Offset refers to the process in which an intermediate roll or cylinder is introduced between the plate cylinder and the impression

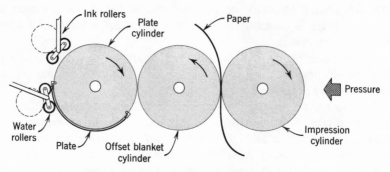

Figure 26.   Principles of an offset press.

cylinder. The offset principle is shown in Figure 26. An offset plate is attached to the plate cylinder and alternately applied with water and ink. The ink on the plate is transferred to the offset blanket cylinder. The blanket impression is again transferred, this time onto paper which is passed between the offset cylinder and the impression cylinder. The offset cylinder is usually covered with some form of rubber blanket. There are several advantages to printing on a rubber blanket first and then transferring the impression on the rubber blanket onto paper instead of printing directly from plate to paper. First, the plates wear better and last longer; second, less water actually reaches the paper; third, the resilience of the rubber blanket allows finer print on coarser paper; and fourth, the printing process is faster.

Offset lithography is performed most economically on rotary presses similar to those discussed in the section on letterpress printing. Both sheet-fed and web-fed presses can be used and perfecting is available.

The modern offset-lithography plate is a thin metallic plate, first processed and then clamped to the plate cylinder. The only essential differences among offset plates are the materials used for the ink-receptive and water-receptive areas. Although the differences seem small, there are many varieties of offset plates, and more are being developed. The different types can be divided into three basic groups: (a) surface plates, (b) deep-etch plates, and (c) bimetal and trimetal plates.

The surface plates are the most popular plates used for catalog printing. They are coated with a light-sensitive substance. When the plate is exposed to bright lights through a negative, the light-sensitive substance hardens whereas in the unexposed areas it remains soft. During plate development the soft areas are washed off and a coating of water-receptive material is added. This completes the division of the plate into the ink-receptive and water-receptive areas needed for offset printing. Surface plates are subject to wear, but good surface plates can be used successfully for long runs (40,000 impressions).

Deep-etch plates are made using film positives during light exposure, rather than using negatives as in surface platemaking. When the plates are developed, the printing surface is etched into the plate surface similar to gravure plates. Deep-etch plates are used for long runs and for exceptionally fine work such as color-process printing. Their cost is somewhat higher than surface plates.

Bimetal and trimetal plates are more durable and better-quality than either surface or deep-etched plates. Their costs, however, are also higher and they are not generally used unless printing runs exceed 100,000 copies.

The platemaking process for offset lithography is similar to photoengraving. The preliminary phases of camera work from exposure through developing, stripping, masking, and opaquing are identical. The individual page negatives are then fixed in flats, the size of the flat depending on the size of the press. The placement of negatives into the flats must be in a particular order. This order is called imposition and is important because: (a) it assures that the right pages back each other, and (b) it is compatible with automatic folding and trimming operations. There are many standard impositions which need not be discussed further. The printer knows which imposition is best suited for catalog printing.

GRAVURE PRINTING

The gravure printing process is the most difficult of the three major printing methods; consequently it is the most expensive. Because of the cost gravure is usually not suited for catalog printing. Gravure is best used when reproducing continuous tones even on cheaper grade papers. Unless the catalog is expensively illustrated with high-quality photographs or the print run does not exceed 150,000, gravure is not practical.

PRINTING SPECIFICATION

The preceding material gives a brief background of the printing processes available today. Of more importance, however, is a method that can be used to purchase printing. The easiest way is to develop a printer's specification sheet. A typical specification sheet is given in Figure 27. Each item in the typical sheet is discussed to give a clear picture of what is intended.

Specification Sheet

Number of Pages (including cover)_____Quantity_____Reprints   Yes   No

Reprint Quantity_____

Stock: Text:_____   Cover:_____

Inks: Text:_____   Cover:_____

Preparation	Additional Information, Drawings, Diagrams
Halftones, square up _____	
Halftones, silhouette or drop out __	
Halftones, vignette _____	
Halftones, combination _____	
Halftones, special effects _____	
Duotones _____	
Screens _____	
Strip-ins _____	
Proofs _____	
Trim size _____	
Paper dummy _____	
Foldouts _____	
Punching _____	
Binding _____	
Shipping information _____	
Job release _____	
Delivery _____	

Figure 27.   Typical printing specification sheet.

Number of Pages

This item certainly sounds simple, but it is surprising how many people confuse sheets with pages. Two pages equal one sheet. Printers buy paper according to the quantity of sheets; therefore be sure the two are not confused. If, for example, the number of sheets is designated rather than the number of pages, the paper cost would be doubled. When counting pages, make sure all pages including front matter and index, are incorporated in the final count.

Quantity

Many people ask for quotations on four, five, or more different quantities. This is ridiculous. You know how many catalogs you are going to distribute, or you should know. Any less should not be ordered. If more are wanted ask for a price on the amount needed and a second price for each additional 500 or 1000. Remember, the price quoted by the printer for additional copies applies only if the quantity is specified at the time of the first printing.

Reprints

Printers often take into consideration the fact that there may be a reprint. If the catalog usually is reprinted, make sure the printer knows. A reprint does not necessarily mean another printing without any changes; if a small number of changes are made it can still be considered a reprint. Indicate the quantity of reprints being considered.

Stock (Text and Cover)

Papermaking is a separate field. Consult with a competent printer or directly with paper manufacturer representatives. Detail exactly what is wanted and expected. Ask for samples and prices. Prices are usually quoted on a weight basis but even this is a guide. It is extremely important that the printer know what paper you want. If he thinks it is not suitable for the job, make another evaluation; otherwise the printer should not be held responsible for poor performance on press. The stock or material for the cover is equally important. Whether the cover material is paper, plastic, cloth, or leather, it must be suited for the cover design.

Inks (Text and Cover)

A particular ink need not be specified—only the color or colors. If a special color is needed, an additional charge is usually made. Swatch books that contain standard color formulas are available. If possible, choose the standards; they have as much impact for considerably less cost. If a specific color is necessary, supply a large sample so that the printer can match it satisfactorily.

Give as many details about the use of additional colors as possible. If colors are used on each page, state this in the specification sheet. The selection of ink types is the printer's responsibility; it is a technical process. Drying time, absorption, and so forth, are too unfamiliar to laymen.

Halftones

Halftones are made from continuous-tone copy, such as photographs and wash drawings. When producing halftones the copy is shot through a glass plate that contains a grid of fine lines. The grid is used to break up the copy into thousands of tiny dots, making it possible to reproduce the copy on a press. The glass plate with the grid of fine lines is called a screen. Screens are available with grids that contain approximately 50 lines an inch to approximately 300. The most popular sizes in this range are 65, 100, 110, 120, 133, and 150. Usually the finer the screen (more grid lines per inch), the finer the quality of reproduction; however, the paper texture is also an important consideration. Figure 28 shows a halftone reproduction in which a variety of screens was used. From the examples it is obvious that the finer screens are more desirable. The screen size is usually selected by the printer, but one should be aware of the expected results.

The typical specification sheet in Figure 27 lists several categories of halftone—square-up, silhouette or drop-out, vignette, special effect, and combination. Each is illustrated in Figure 29.

The square-up halftone has both the subject and background screened and is the most economical method of producing halftone illustrations. The silhouette or drop-out halftone eliminates the screened background, leaving only the subject. This usually is accomplished by an artist carefully opaquing the background during the negative stage. This is a cost that can be controlled somewhat during the preparation of the continuous-tone copy. If a silhouette is desired, the artist should apply white repro paint around the outside edges of the copy. This provides sharp contrast between subject and background; good camera work can take care of the rest.

A vignette halftone has a screened background around the subject that fades away into the white of the paper. Combination halftones refer to illustrations that contain both continuous-tone and line copy. Information on producing reproducible copy for this type of illustration is given in Chapter 7.

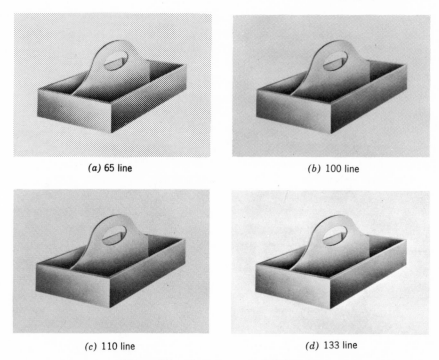

(a) 65 line   (b) 100 line

(c) 110 line   (d) 133 line

Figure 28.   Typical screened halftones.

The last halftone shown in Figure 29 is called a special-effect halftone. The screens used do not have the standard grid pattern but circular patterns. Straight or wavy line patterns are also available. This type of halftone is becoming more popular, but not especially for catalog printing. It could be used for printing a cover illustration since it provides an interesting reproduction.

Duotones

Duotones can be classified as special-effect halftones, although they differ somewhat from the ones just discussed. Duotones, as the name implies, use two tones in a screened halftone. This is accomplished by using two screens with grids slighty offset from each other. The screens are produced on separate negatives; therefore during the printing process, different colors can be used to print each set of dots. This is a delicate process and care must be exercised so moire patterns are not formed. The use of duotones results in more distinctive reproduction. Because a double operation is necessary to obtain this effect, there is a cost factor

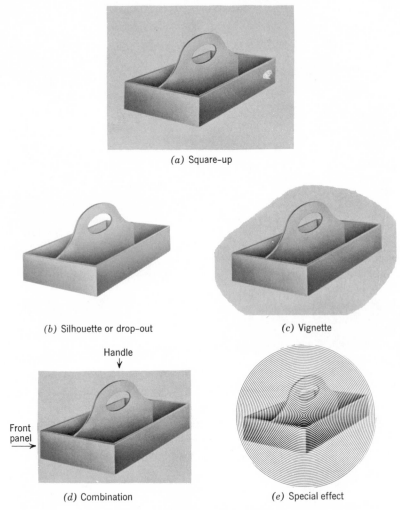

(a) Square-up

(b) Silhouette or drop-out

(c) Vignette

(d) Combination

(e) Special effect

Figure 29.   Various types of halftone.

that must be considered. An economical method of obtaining a duotone effect is to print one color (black, for example) on tinted stock.

Screens

Screens, often called bendays, can be added to line copy to soften the presentation. As shown in Figure 30, screens must be identified by

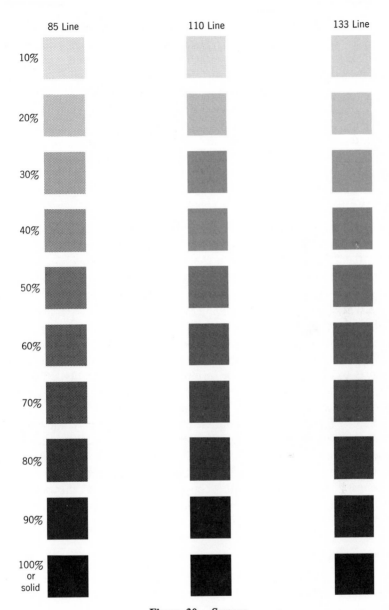

Figure 30. Screens.

their size and the percentage of darkness (tint). The tint is specified in percentages of a solid color. A typical use for a screen is to drop back the harshness of a solid black border around catalog tabular matter. No special preparation is necessary when the reproducible copy is being prepared. Simply add to the printer's instructions the size and percentage of screen required.

If a panel of screening is desired to provide emphasis or bleed indexing, the area to be screened must be clearly identified, preferably on a separate overlay. Printer's instructions must be added to delineate the screen size and percentage.

Strip-Ins

Strip-ins, or stripping, is the name of the process of combining line negatives with halftones; it may also refer to the placement of page negatives in flats. Strip-ins represent a significant cost factor because stripping is a time-consuming job. Extreme care must be exercised when stripping screened negatives in place to avoid mistakes; an illustration can easily be placed incorrectly and occasionally even upside down.

Although stripping is the most common method of obtaining photographic reproductions, there is a trend toward using reduced, screened positive photostats on the reproducible line copy. Although there is some resistance to this method in the printing trade, the quality of screened positive photostats has improved so that they can be used for catalogs. Their main advantage is cost; the printer requires no strip-in time. He can take one line shot of the complete page (assuming one-color printing). Another advantage is that the designer knows that all illustrations are in proper place. The reviewer, who gives final catalog approval, has an opportunity to see the completed page before it is printed. This procedure can be used when screening line copy; in other words, the designer is actually preparing screened reproducible copy. Question the printer about this procedure; get his opinion; ask for samples.

Proofs

Proofs are available in many forms. They are used as a final check of the catalog before printing. Proofs should be circulated to and approved by the persons designated as the approval authority. Although any changes made at this time are costly, errors should be corrected. Printer's proofs may be referred to as salt prints, Van Dykes, or press proofs. Special proofs, called 3M or progressive proofs, should be supplied if additional colors are used. A set of proofs are made showing each color separately and combined. The cost of proofs is relatively inexpensive and at least two complete copies should be ordered. Specify the number of copies and the type desired.

Trim Size

Trim size refers to the page size intended for the printed catalog. The most standard size is $8\frac{1}{2}'' \times 11''$; it should be used except when a good reason exists for deviation. Trim size should also be given for the cover. If the cover material is heavy, you may want it to extend slightly over the paper; this offers some protection to the catalog pages. The overhang should not be great or the cover will develop a tendency to curve or "dog ear."

Paper Dummy

It is always advisable to obtain a paper dummy of the catalog from the printer before printing actually begins. If the catalog program is properly planned, this should have been done in the planning stage. The paper dummy gives the exact catalog bulking. Catalog bulking determines shipping, mailing, and distribution costs. Bulking must be considered during paper selection; sometimes it is desirable to use heavy paper that will increase bulk and give the illusion of a larger catalog. You must know the size of the printed catalog.

Foldouts

If the catalog contains foldout pages (pages that are longer than the standard page size), information on the number and individual sizes must be included. The use of foldout pages in a catalog should be discouraged. In most cases the subject matter can be condensed or presented in a different manner to eliminate the need for a foldout page. One method is to use two-page spreads. Foldout pages are expensive to reproduce and drastically affect the cost of the over-all printing job. If foldout pages are required to get the message across properly, by all means use them; otherwise try to eliminate them.

Punching and Binding

These two items must be compatible. Normally, saddle-stitched, perfect-bound, or case-bound catalogs are not punched. Mechanical binding, such as wire, loose-leaf, and GBC, requires that the catalog be punched to accommodate the binding. There are many punching patterns from which to select. Investigate them.

Shipping Information

Often adequate shipping instructions are not given to the printer; therefore he will quote f.o.b. his plant. This fact might be overlooked when reviewing printing quotations. If so, shipping charges must be paid. When the end of the catalog program is near, the catalog budget may be almost depleted. Make a positive statement on delivery in the printing specification. Investigate the possibility of having the printer ship bulk quantities to distributors and representatives. If storage is a problem, many of the larger printers offer reasonable storage rates. If large quantities of catalogs are being printed, delivery logistics become an important factor, also a costly one.

Another consideration is catalog packing. If catalogs are large, make sure that the quantity per carton is reasonable so that a packed carton will not be too heavy. Sometimes female employees are responsible for the mailing and distribution functions. If cartons are too heavy for them to handle, an additional problem is created. Do not take shipment for granted. If properly planned, it can be done efficiently; if not, it becomes a sizable task.

Job Release

An accurate prediction of job release is important to the printer. Remember, he is selling press time. The larger the job, the more important this becomes. For large jobs an early authorization should be given so that the printer can order paper in advance. The lead time on large paper orders can be the most significant factor in the delivery date of the printed catalogs.

Delivery

The delivery date to you is as important as the job-release date to the printer. This is particularly true of larger jobs for which a distribution crew must be formed to mail the catalogs. Slippage in the release date results in slippage in the delivery date. Therefore these dates must be established after all aspects of the program have been carefully considered.

COLOR-PROCESS PRINTING

Before ending the chapter on printing, a brief discussion of color-process printing is given. This is the process used to reproduce colored illustrations, such as a colored photograph. Color-process printing is much more than the mechanical color-separating process previously discussed. A rule of thumb on color-process printing is that a set of four-process plates costs approximately 20 times a single color plate. This should not inhibit one from using full-color illustrations if they are necessary. It is intended only to make one aware of the cost factor so that plans can be made.

Basically, platemaking requires three distinct operations, each of which must be performed properly or the printed results will be poor. In the first operation color separation is performed using special lenses. The number of lenses depends on the quality desired. Usually, four lenses are used, one for each of the three primary colors and a fourth for black which adds contrast and depth to the printed illustration.

Color correction must be performed next. This is a delicate operation that requires considerable time. Skilled craftsmen are used to perform color correction. After this step the plates are press proved. This indicates whether additional correction is needed or whether the plates are satisfactory for the final printing.

There is new electronic color-scanning equipment that performs color separation automatically, thus eliminating the time-consuming, hand corrections previously required. This equipment is quite expensive and only larger printers can afford them.

A special technique is used when making colored plates. Each color must be slightly offset from each other so the eye can blend them to reproduce the original full-colored image. To offset the dot patterns, halftone screens are placed at different angles for each color. If properly done, this eliminates the disturbing moire patterns that otherwise are present.

When checking process-color proofs, compare them with the original copy for proper color balance. Imbalances can be corrected in two ways— by correcting the plates or by changing ink colors slightly. These are delicate operations that the printer should perform.

9

DISTRIBUTION AND MAINTENANCE

After catalog printing, distribution is the next major milestone. How do catalogs gets into the hands of potential customers? The catalog maintenance factor becomes a problem only when the catalog is no longer up-to-date or does not reflect an entire line. This factor is influenced chiefly by the nature of a business. Unfortunately, domestic-type catalogs have an extremely short life due to ever-changing trends in fashion. The continuous surge of world technology also has caused fast obsolescence of technical catalogs.

DISTRIBUTION

The distribution of most printed catalogs should be made through your existing marketing structure; for example, if you have nationwide or worldwide distributors and representatives, bulk shipments should be sent to them for individual distribution. The most effective distribution method is to have a salesman or representative make a personal call to deliver the catalog. This gives him another opportunity to confront a potential customer and display his wares. Obviously, if the catalog distribution list is too large, this is impossible.

The most economical method to distribute large quantities of catalogs is by fourth-class mail. For large mailings it is mandatory to use some form of automatic addressing equipment, such as the popular Addressograph machine. If you are not equipped with this machinery, inquire about this service through your printer. There are many companies who specialize in direct-mail services and are equipped with the automatic machinery necessary to provide economical service. An important item in mail distribution is the buildup and maintenance of good mailing lists. Lists can be made and catalogs distributed geographically, by professional breakdown or other pertinent categories to obtain the best response.

If the basic catalog distribution is by mail, individual packaging is necessary to protect the catalog from the abuses of service. The quality of the exterior wrapping or envelope depends on the catalog covers. Paper or plastic covers require more protection than hard-bound catalogs. Various attempts have been made to achieve maximum protection at the lowest possible cost. The most successful method is the corrugated paper carton with "bumper edges" for absorbing shock. This type of carton is shown in Figure 31. The bumper edges offer substantial protection to the corners of the catalog. Book corners are subjected to the most abuse in mailing. If this packaging is used, it should be sealed simply. If not, the catalog could be damaged if the recipient cuts into it while breaking the seal. Hard-bound catalogs can be packed in the more conventional type of carton.

The outer surface of the carton should identify the contents. There has been much energy, effort, and money expended to obtain the printed catalog. Do not stop here. For best results the carton should have an attractive design. When planning the carton design, you must take into consideration the weight of the corrugated paper. Generally, there are two weights used for mailing bound literature—general purpose 200-pound test and the extra-heavy duty 275-pound test. Standard colors are tan and white. Printing can be performed on the corrugated paper by using soft rubber plates. Check this restriction with the printer and make sure the carton design is compatible with his equipment.

Often an interior wrap is used to provide additional protection. This

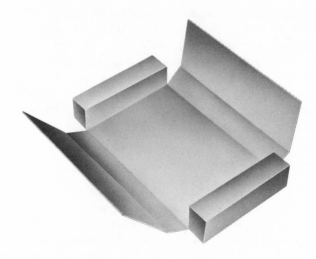

Figure 31.   Bumper-edge carton.

could be tissue paper in the most economical form or the catalog could be encased and heat-sealed in a plastic bag which would be the most expensive method. Psychologically, plastic encasement adds character, distinction, and importance to a catalog. Depending on quantities, this feature could cost from one to three cents per copy, so although it is desirable, it may not be practical. Such items often depend on the company image you are trying to project. Many people think that a company's image is invaluable whereas others say it is worthless. Anything said here will not completely satisfy arguments on either side. A secondary advantage to plastic encasement is that it adds to the storage life of the catalog. This may not be a factor if the catalog is continuously reissued or changed.

Which method should be used for distributing the catalog? Weigh all factors before deciding. Never lose sight of the fact that the purpose of the catalog is to sell products. This is the reason for business and the only reason for staying in business. Anything that increases the chances for more sales is justified. There is, however, a practical limit that must be weighed. The means that justify the results must be economically practical. Whether catalog distribution is through the personal contact of the sales force or through the mails must be decided after considering your particular conditions. Both will work, if effectively implemented.

DISTRIBUTION FOLLOW-UP

Many times there is no follow-up system after catalog distribution. The attitude might be, we prepared, printed, and distributed it; let's sit back and await the orders. No effective marketing system can ever afford to remain inactive. Remember, the catalog is a key item in a marketing structure. An active follow-up system gives another legitimate reason to approach potential customers and say "you see what I have for you." Catalog follow-up is part of coordinating the catalog with the over-all marketing plan. This is discussed in more detail in Chapter 10.

CATALOG MAINTENANCE

Catalog maintenance or up-dating is a problem that must be considered during preparation of the initial edition. How long will the material included in the catalog remain valid? What is the nature of your business? If the rapid product changes are a part of your business life, the catalog program must be geared to this operation. There are three methods available to up-date a catalog—revisions, reissues, and new editions. Each will be discussed critically.

Revisions

Revision is a general term used to describe changes required to up-date a book. In the context of this discussion it is meant to identify the process of up-dating a catalog by using anything but a complete reprinting; for example, errata pages or a set of change pages are considered revisions. An errata sheet is a tabulation of simple corrections. A typical entry on an errata page might be: "page 29 change refrigerator width from 28 to 31"." When using the change-page system, a new page 29 is supplied showing the corrected dimension of the refrigerator.

For either of these systems to be practical the catalog must be bound in some form of loose-leaf; that is, pages must be easily removed and inserted. If a catalog is not bound in this manner, these systems should not be used.

There is one major argument against these systems of catalog maintenance; that is, you must impose on your customers to make the changes. In most cases it can be taken for granted that they will not bother doing it and either throw away or misplace the corrected material. Any time that you impose on persons, a negative reaction is created immediately. This certainly will not help sales. There are, however, counterarguments that favor the use of errata sheets or change pages. The most important is cost. Using either of these methods is much more economical than reprinting and redistributing corrected or up-dated catalogs. Can you afford this economy at the expense of customer goodwill? This question must be answered before deciding on these methods. A second argument in favor of using errata sheets and correction pages is that it affords still another opportunity to contact customers. Persistent customer contact has its merits when handled properly? Also, publicly admitting mistakes is an admirable quality. When these factors are applied to correcting a catalog, however, they can do nothing but hurt company image for they suggest a certain amount of uncertainty and lack of quality.

Errata sheets or correction pages should be used only as a last resort to up-date catalogs and then only if the corrected sheets or pages can be easily inserted and the old ones removed.

Reissue

When should a catalog be reissued? To answer this question, first another question must be answered—why reissue a catalog? Generally, a reissue is required when the catalog is no longer doing the job for which it was produced. Sales records are the best yardsticks. Another factor is the amount of new products produced since the last catalog was distributed. Are they important enough to justify the cost of a catalog reissue? Remember, brochures can serve as effective stopgaps until enough new products are produced to make it practical to reissue the catalog.

Just what is a reissue? In the contents of this discussion a reissue is a new catalog that contains a majority of the material included in an existing catalog. In other words if fifty percent or more of the existing catalog material is valid, the cost of up-dating the catalog can be reduced considerably by planning the new material around the valid material. This is particularly true if the existing catalog was well-received. When publishing a reissue always make a significant change on the cover. This is a simple method of immediately telling anyone using the new catalog, who is familiar with the old one, that he has an up-to-date one. It is advisable to keep some resemblance to tie the new and old catalogs together, although generally this is accomplished by the company's name and logo. It is also advisable to send with the catalog reissue a notice that states that this issue replaces the existing one and a suggestion to discard the old issue to avoid confusion in the future. This can be done very tactfully. Here again you make it easier on yourself by making it easier for your clients.

One particularly annoying problem that must be confronted in publishing a reissue is the effect the new material has on consecutive page numbers. Often new material is added near the front of the catalog which upsets the entire numbering sequence. If the catalog is in sections, the best method of combating this problem is to use section page numbers in the original issue. This requires the use of a two-part page number; for example, the first page in each of the sections in a five-section catalog would be 1-1, 2-1, 3-1, 4-1, and 5-1. This method is simple, logical, and yet does not impose serious problems on the usefulness of the catalog. In fact it provides a subtle method of catalog indexing for the first number identifies the section. Using this method means that if a change is made or material is added to one section, only the page numbers of that section are affected. All other catalog page numbers remain unchanged. The existing printing plates or negatives of the unchanged sections are still valid and can be used, and there is no need to touch the page mechanicals.

Although new pages will change the printer's imposition, the over-all savings in copy preparation and new negatives are significant. Creating a new page imposition which fits the new catalog is a relatively simple task for the printer.

When all the factors just discussed are considered, you should have the answer to the question—when do you reissue a catalog? A reissue is probably the best solution when weighing the economics and desired results of up-dating the catalog. No one is upset when they receive a reissue. This implies that you have taken the customer's best interest into consideration and want to keep them completely up-to-date.

When estimating the cost of a reissue, you must consider the research, writing, illustrating, and production factors to produce the new or corrected material plus printing the entire catalog. The final cost is the redistribution. Accurate records on the initial distribution will provide the exact costs of the new distribution. Although the costs of reissuing a catalog certainly are higher than those needed to produce errata sheets or change pages, the catalog should be reissued when changes and corrections justify the presence of new material in the field. Favorable customer reaction to this versus the corrected sheets far outweighs the additional costs. Also, if the existing catalog is not loose-leaf, it is the only practical method of providing limited changes.

New Editions

How does a new edition differ from a catalog reissue? It differs simply in the quantity of material that must be changed. If a majority of the material in the existing catalog is obsolete, a new edition is required. Attempting to salvage a small percent of material that is valid is false economy. If the nature of your business has created this situation, a new catalog with a new approach certainly is justified. This is particularly true in the fast-changing, domestic markets today. There is continuous demand for new style, different colors, and additional coveniences which must be met. These changes must be reflected in up-to-date catalog material.

A new edition affords the opportunity to change the catalog to reflect field suggestions for improvements. These suggestions must always be thoroughly evaluated and incorporated if possible. The suggestions may be not only in content but also in format and organization. Preparing a new edition is to begin again. Although it is simply stated, it is a very significant cost factor. The need for new catalog material in the field must be great enough to justify a new edition.

Although a new edition is a costly venture, it should never be considered a necessary evil. Many companies today are highly successful using only their catalog as its sales force. Catalogs are an important and necessary tool in an effective marketing program. Do not let yours become so antiquated that it is a source of annoyance to clients. When a change is in order and can be justified, it must be made as expeditiously as possible.

SUMMARY

Catalog distribution and maintenance are significant cost factors that must be considered when establishing a budget for a catalog program. These are costly but necessary; their costs emphasize further the importance of accuracy when initially preparing catalog material. The costs of checking and rechecking are far less than those that may be necessary to correct an error once the catalog is published and distributed. In addition there is always the immeasurable factor of customer ill will created by erroneous material in the field.

10

CATALOG COORDINATION WITH MARKETING PLANS

Catalogs that are isolated in an over-all marketing plan lose their tremendous sales potential and weaken over-all marketing effectiveness. A large investment is made to produce, print, and distribute a good, informative catalog; it is apparent then that all efforts should be made to obtain the most from it. The biggest portion of the job is finished, catalogs are in all known, potential customers' offices. You must now motivate them to use it. Do not sit back and wait for the orders. There are ways of making potential customers more aware of the catalog than simply having it somewhere in their offices; for example, advertising, salesmen, distributors, representatives, and mailing pieces have a common denominator. They are continuously contacting customers. Each provides an opportunity to make people aware of your catalog. Make tactful use of all facilities.

ADVERTISEMENTS

Advertising is a field in itself. Normally, its main function is to create interest or to motivate. Advertisements can go only so far. When properly placed, they make thousands of contacts daily. Advertisements make known what you are selling and direct attention toward a particular feature of your products. To obtain greater value from your advertising budget and at the same time promote the use of your catalog, simply include a statement that additional information is available in the catalog. Also include instructions on obtaining a catalog. Just this simple action, if repeated often enough, will increase the chances that your catalog will be used or requested the next time a need for your type of products arises. Acknowledge the existence of the catalog in every advertisement you place. It costs no more and sells plenty.

SALESMEN, DISTRIBUTORS, AND REPRESENTATIVES

Ample supplies of the catalog should be available to your salesmen, distributors, and representatives. They must be urged to acknowledge the existence of your catalog at every opportunity. Having a salesman show potential customers what is in the catalog can make an effective sales presentation. He can explain how it is used, how it is indexed, how it can benefit the client, and how easy it is to order or specify products. A catalog also provides a salesman with an attractive door opener. Most people are curious and will see a salesman if he has something to hand out. Successful salesmen will take advantage of such an opportunity for the importance of personal contact cannot be overemphasized in selling. Here again the cost of this program is negligible. You have salesmen, they do make calls, so why not recruit and teach them the importance of the catalog as a sales tool. It will help them in the long run. If a potential customer calls a salesman because of an interesting item in the catalog, chances are fairly good that the salesman will make a sale. It is vitally important that the salesman be thoroughly familiar with the catalog. The worst possible impression is made if he fumbles through the catalog to find something in response to an inquiry. The faster he finds the answer, the more impressive he and the catalog are. This action cannot help but promote the use of your catalog and products. The salesman and catalog should complement each other for best results on the sales graphs.

DIRECT MAIL

Direct mail is the second largest advertising medium used today (newspapers are first). Unfortunately much of this has little impact for it is not being used properly. Direct-mail advertisements have one important advantage over other forms of advertisements. They can be directed to a selected group, the group most interested in your products or services. Space advertisements, whether they are in newspaper, radio, television, or magazines, provide much broader coverage. Often an analogy is made—shotgun (advertisement) versus rifle (direct mail). Match your business with your advertising medium. But more important, whatever medium you use, always promote the catalog by mentioning it. Make people continuously cognizant of the fact that one exists.

Most space advertisements include inquiry cards. These should be answered promptly and not with form letters. Generally, if a person takes the time to fill out an inquiry card and mail it, he is interested in your products. It is up to you to find out exactly what is his interest. All inquiries must be followed up. The best start, especially if a general inquiry is received, is to send a catalog along with a letter of thanks for the interest expressed. If there is an effective marketing plan, you will not stop here. Do not depend entirely on the catalog. Establish an active follow-up plan with salesmen, distributors, and representatives.

If direct-mail advertising is most appropriate for your business, gear for it and implement it properly. There are many companies that specialize in direct-mail selling. If you are not equipped for direct-mail advertising, call a competent supplier and see what he can offer. Be certain that all mail contains some reference to the catalog.

There are several different materials that can be used effectively in a direct-mail campaign or, many times, by themselves. They include leaflets, brochures, published technical notes, and product releases.

Leaflets

Leaflets are usually single sheets (two pages) or double sheets (four pages) that are used to best advantage to emphasize a particular product or feature. They are relatively inexpensive to produce and help keep potential clients informed of latest product developments. Full-color presentations should be used to provide eye-catching appeal. The actual marketing impact or purchasing motivation of leaflets is difficult to predict or measure. They do provide an inexpensive method of keeping the company's name in front of clients. Because you are trying to make a lasting impression on clients, the leaflets should be produced tastefully. Thus if an impression is made, it will be favorable.

Brochures

Brochures or pamphlets can be used·effectively in an over-all marketing plan and can also support or complement the catalog. A brochure can be considered a small catalog; there is no clear distinction in page count that distinguishes a brochure from a catalog. Generally, brochures are produced with multiples of four pages; that is 4, 8, 12, 16, 20, and so forth. Because of their smaller size, the preparation, production, and printing cycles of brochures are considerably shorter than those of larger catalogs.

Brochures are used to best advantage to emphasize specific product lines. This is particularly true if there is a broad line of products. Market-specialized brochures provide economical coverage for limited-market products. A brochure will feature these products in proper perspective whereas they may go unnoticed in a large catalog. Also, as discussed earlier, smaller catalogs or brochures are easier to use simply because they have less pages to search through to find an item of interest.

If catalogs are sectionalized, brochures can be developed more economically. Proper planning during the preparation of the catalog may allow for direct use of catalog reproducible materials in the preparation of the brochure. Although good planning is essential, in order to make reuse of catalog material possible, an introduction or transition is necessary to convert catalog pages into a successful brochure. A cover should be designed especially for the brochure. It should have a family resemblance to the catalog cover to provide a degree of harmony and unity. The brochure should also contain a brief message on other product lines and mention the existence of the general catalog.

Brochures can also be used as stopgaps between catalog printings. If a new product is developed and the timing of the next catalog will not give the immediate marketing coverage that is desirable, the brochure provides an economical yet satisfactory solution. Because of the timing problem, reproducible copy for the brochure should be developed so it can be used in the next catalog.

Technical Notes

Technical notes can be used for many reasons. Many companies publish and circulate technical notes that discuss typical and unusual applications of their products. The obvious benefit is that those who receive the technical notes may recognize an application they might need. A potential sale is found.

Another popular use of technical notes is to keep interested parties informed of latest research developments. This indirectly creates motivation through the power of suggestion, and it arouses curiosity. The technical notes should contain some instruction for the curious to investigate. It is an ideal spot to mention the general catalog or simply to solicit a mail or telephone inquiry. Obtaining an inquiry immediately increases chances for a sale.

The function of technical notes, as the name implies, is to provide a means of getting interesting technical information to interested parties. Technical notes are more effective if they are produced by a standard format; this ties them together and to your company. Company identification among potential clients is an important goal in any marketing program. Establishing a series of periodical literature with a standard format helps accomplish this goal. It also reduces the costs necessary for their production. Many companies provide loose-leaf binders with their technical notes so that recipients can conveniently collect and save them.

Catalog material can be subtly added to technical notes. You are again given an opportunity of telling potential clients about your catalog.

Product Releases

A major source of product publicity, other than those mentioned above, is the product release. A good release effectively supplements all other forms of advertising. Many small companies depend on product releases as their only form of publicity.

Industrial, trade, and business magazines usually provide a "what's new," "new equipment," or "new products" page or section in the publication. Normally, this space is offered without charge. Product release pages are quite popular, and many persons with specific problems scan these pages looking for an advancement or new development in the "state of the art." Usually the space allotted for product releases is small; therefore to prepare the best product release keep copy brief and to the point. Include the most significant basic particulars. This is the most effective way to stimulate interest. Also when a trade magazine permits, include a photograph. This is the best way to substantiate the existence of the new product. In concluding the copy for the product release solicit inquiries about the new product and offer a free general catalog. Offering a free catalog is not always wise. This often puts the request on a bingo-card that may produce thousands of requests from nonprospects. The decision must be made on the basis of your particular circumstances.

When preparing the product release material, it is important to know how much space the magazine editor will allow. Ask him for specifics. Do not submit more material than space allows. If too much copy is submitted the door is opened for magazine editors to apply editorial red pencils to your copy. When they are finished the copy may not emphasize the points you think are most pertinent.

The importance of product releases cannot be overemphasized. Are you taking full advantage of this economical service? Are you placing product releases in all trade magazines in your field? If not, you are losing an extremely valuable communications channel to potential clients.

CONTESTS

The increasing popularity of contest marketing programs is a recent development. The use of contests is normally restricted to domestic markets and finds little or no use in technical and construction fields. The continuous success of this type of program cannot be ignored. There are two extreme reactions to contests designed for selling—reception or suspicion. Why a person is more interested in a half-bill of play money rather than the quality of the product he is purchasing remains a mystery of human behavior. Certainly, not all persons fall into this category. It is gratifying to know that some people are still looking for their money's worth and are uninterested in the give-away programs. Sound business must be based on quality products. This encourages repeated business which further emphasizes the importance of good products.

The above statement are not offered as an indictment against contest programs. Many times a company is forced in this direction by competition which is the key to our free-enterprise system. Adequately combating competition is the function of a marketing department. The best method is to stay ahead of competition. Do not be a follower; be a leader. If careful evaluation of your over-all marketing plan clearly shows that contest programs will best suit your promotion needs, use them.

If you do not have the in-house capability of implementing a contest program, there are many competent public relations agencies that have been supplying this service for years. Call several of them and ask for presentations before selecting one.

Contests sometimes can be designed with the use of the catalog a requirement. In other words an answer may be found only in the catalog, making it necessary for contestants to pick up and use it. This obviously has limited applications but is a possibility.

11

CATALOGS AND COMPUTERS

HISTORY

The use of high-speed computers for preparing reproducible materials is becoming increasingly popular in the publishing field. Presently, computers do not provide composition in the normal sense that they convert manuscript copy into copy suitable for printing or for direct platemaking. The most common use of computers for composition is the automatic justification of lines. The computer justifies lines at a much faster rate than can possibly be accomplished manually. The computer justifies lines at a much faster rate than can possibly be accomplished manually.

Even when using a computer, the manuscript must be manually retyped on a keyboard machine. The keyboard machine is similar to a typewriter and normally produces a punched tape. A second type of keyboard machine, which is discussed later in this chapter, produces magnetic tape. During this typing the operator need not be concerned with line justification. The punched tape can be proofed rapidly by running it through a print-out machine and obtaining a proofreader's copy. The print-out may create some proofreading difficulty. The lines are still unjustified and special computer symbols are present on the print and proof copy. This type of copy is confusing to the untrained eye. The proof stage can be bypassed completely and final justified copy can be produced. This, however, eliminates the economy of making corrections at the earliest stages. A workable compromise might be to have the printer's proofreader check the first proof print-out and the writer check the justified proof print-out. As future developments and refinements are made, computers and print-out machines will be designed to produce a conventional, readable, justified proof copy on the first run through which compares to the galley proofs obtained in standard typesetting operations.

For the computer to provide justified copy it must be instructed properly to perform exactly what is desired. In computer language this form of

115

instruction is called programming. Programming is a specialized art which has a direct bearing on the effectiveness of the computer for producing copy. As discussed later in this chapter, the time required for programming the computer has a direct bearing on whether computer composition will be the most economical method of providing justified copy.

Normally, the advantages of the high-speed computer operation is severely limited by the relatively low speed of the keyboard machine operator. Even the keyboard machine is capable of operating much faster than humanly possible. This fact cannot be overcome. But to obtain full advantage from the high-speed computer, several keyboard machines must be used to feed it. So far, only the inputs to the computer are discussed. At the output side the same basic problem exists; one computer is capable of keeping many typesetting machines busy. One solution to this has been the development of the Linofilm process discussed later in this chapter.

A major advantage of computer operations for producing justified copy is the fast rate that corrections can be made. The first proof copy is read and any corrections are typed out on the keyboard machine which produces another tape. This tape along with the first is fed into the computer. The computer automatically matches the two with the information on the correction tape overriding the material on the first tape. The result is a third tape which is the corrected and justified master tape. The master tape either can be punched or magnetic depending on the composing equipment in the system.

The justification process is a relatively simple task for the computer. The Justowriter machine discussed in Chapter 2 is in many respects a simple computer because it produces justified copy. Computers can be provided that complete other more complicated tasks automatically. One outstanding example is proper word division. A Justowriter machine, for example, must have an operator present to cope with word-division problems. The larger and more expensive computers provide fully automatic justification with automatic word division. Even this arrangement is not always practical since many grammarians are hopelessly split on the division of certain words. The capability of word division adds tremendously to the size of the computer for it must have memory devices to store huge volumes of information. In some cases a complete dictionary is stored in memory devices.

The computer industry has attempted to resolve the problem of word division by publishing a standard for hyphenation. This standard should be available to you from most companies providing computer composition services.

To provide some feeling for the required steps that are necessary for computer composition, the Linofilm process is discussed below. Computer research is being made continuously so that all steps can be performed by one machine in one operation. This is a noteworthy goal which it is safe to say is still years away. Even when this development takes place, there is an obvious weakness that will remain for the machine will require a perfect plan at the outset of the program. Because human behavior is the main factor to be considered in the preparation of an initial plan, it would be rare indeed if the first plan were the best plan. This simply is not the nature of publishing, for many persons must team up to produce a top-quality publication.

A computer that will produce not only the justified copy but also the halftone and line artwork is being developed. In other words, illustrative material as well as the copy would be inserted, possibly by electronic scanning, and programmed for proper size and location. The computer output would be reproducible pages (or negatives) suitable for direct use by the printer. Future developments will be interesting to observe, and if you think you can apply this service inquire about the latest refinements from competent suppliers. Obtain quotations and compare them against more conventional methods of producing typeset reproducible copy.

THE LINOFILM COMPUTER PROCESS

The Linofilm computer process is selected for discussion because presently it appears to be best suited for catalog composition.

There are four basic steps to be performed: (a) preparing proof copy, (b) master tape, (c) film positives, and (d) final corrections. Each is discussed below.

Proof Copy

The keyboard machines in the Linofilm process often are called tapewriters. Tapewriters have a standard typewriter keyboard plus additional symbols and commands that are required by the computer; for example, if a heading is to be in boldface, a command symbol must be punched into the tape by the tapewriter. As shown in Figure 32, several tapewriters can be used to type manuscript copy. The tapes produced by the tapewriter are fed into a paper tape reader which converts the punched information into electronic signals required by the computer. The computer digests and processes this material and sorts it in accordance with its program. The program consists basically of column width. The computer in turn feeds a high-speed printer and a magnetic storage unit. The high-speed

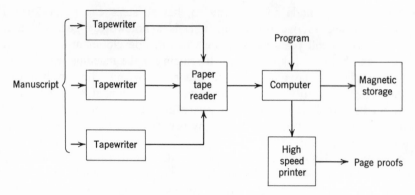

Figure 32.   Preparing Linofilm proof copy.

printer actually prints out the proof pages to be proofread. The storage unit accepts the computer information and magnetically stores it so that it can be retrieved easily upon receipt of the proper command. This completes the proof-copy preparation phase of the Linofilm process.

Master Tape

As shown in Figure 33, all corrections, whether proofreader's or equipment changes, must be typed on the tapewriter. This correction tape is then fed into the paper tape reader which functions as described above during the proof copy phase. The computer in addition to receiving the new or corrected material from the tape receives the old information from the magnetic storage unit. The computer rapidly makes the comparisons and produces a master tape that includes all corrected material. The computer handles all the timing necessary for this operation. It also produces retrieval commands that are applied to the magnetic storage unit. These commands dictate to the storage unit what information the computer wants and when it wants it. Pagination information also can

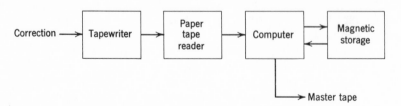

Figure 33.   Preparing Linofilm master copy.

be added during this phase by using the tapewriter. This completes the second phase of the Linofilm operation, the preparation of the master tape.

Film Positive

The next step in the Linofilm process is the preparation of the film positive. This is illustrated in Figure 34. The master tape produced by most computers is normally a six-channel tape. The photocomposition tape required by most Linofilm photocomposition units is a fifteen-channel tape. The main purpose of the paper tape converter is to accept the six-channel tape from the computer and produce a fifteen-channel tape that is compatible with the Linofilm photocomposition unit. The photocomposition unit produces the film positives that are used to prepare final page mechanicals.

Before continuing it should be noted that the process discussed produces reproducible galleys. It can be programmed to produce complete page make-up, except for illustrations, if this is desirable. To provide this additional function, additional computer programming is necessary. This programming can become involved and time-consuming. A certain balance must be maintained to keep computer composition economical and competitive. If the programming becomes too involved, all price advantages are lost.

Final Corrections

Final corrections can be made on a Linofilm keyboard if they are required. This provides an economical method of making minor corrections at a very late stage in the composition process. If changes or corrections are extensive at this point, the entire procedure should be repeated. This may sound like a tremendous task, but remember the magnetic storage unit has all the data stored magnetically. Only the corrections need be typed and inserted into the system. The magnetic storage unit has all the text material in the catalog available on retrieval. The Linofilm keyboard used to make final corrections often is referred to as the composer because it can splice corrected film into the original film.

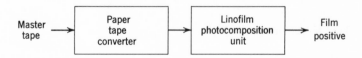

Figure 34.   Preparing Linofilm positives.

This completes the discussion of the Linofilm composition process, but it certainly does not complete the work of producing a catalog. Page mechanicals must be made from the film positives, as explained in Chapter 7. As already mentioned, Linofilm is not the only computer composition process available today. It represents a more practical method for catalogs. If you think you can use computer composition for your catalog, do not feel restricted to the Linofilm process. Investigate suppliers of other computer methods; the important factor is the end result, not the methods of obtaining it. This assumes that the economic factor is basically equal. When weighing economics, do not forget to include the time you spend handling and processing these data.

MAGNETIC TAPE CONTROLLED DIRECT IMPRESSION TYPOGRAPHY

The most recent development in computer typography is the magnetic tape-controlled, direct-impression typography system. In this system the manuscript is typed on a standard keyboard machine that produces copy for proofreading purposes as well as a magnetic tape. Corrections are made by retyping the line in which the correction appears. Both the original and correction tape are then fed into a computer composer. The composer operator must enter the basic composing instructions on a control panel and select and insert the proper font. Available type faces include Press Roman, Aldine Roman, Bodoni Book, Univers, and Pyramid. Others are planned for the immediate future.

The composer control panel permits the operator to set copy tight or loose, to compose with or without hyphenation, to select line length and line character count, and to simplify paragraph indention. To change type faces or to switch to boldface for paragraph headings the operator must stop the composer at the control panel. The composer can be operated manually if desired.

The composer manufacturer is confident that the direct-impression system is a serious challenge to hot-metal composition. With continuous development of new fonts and system refinements, it could happen. Cost comparisons at present tend to favor the direct-impression system. It will be interesting to see how the hot-metal industry responds to this challenge.

COMPUTER APPLICATIONS

A computer can be programmed to do many things. Unfortunately, it must be programmed by humans, and if catalog page layouts are complicated programming can become the most significant cost factor. Thus it should be recognized that computer applications for preparing catalogs must be chosen carefully. The original economy of the high-speed computer operation may be offset completely by the extra programming requirements of complex page layouts. A straightforward listing, such as a catalog price list, is an excellent example of a computer application that could be most economical. In a price list the basic format and page content remain similar making the programming function relatively easy.

SUMMARY

Computer service is expensive; therefore the savings it produces must be balanced against its costs. When a single program can be used for many pages in a large catalog, the economy is substantial. This situation is relatively rare in most forms of book publishing and even more so in sales catalogs. It is very difficult to establish general guidelines to determine what catalog tasks should be performed by computer composition and what tasks should not. This is particularly true because of the fantastic amount of research and development that is being made in this field. A major breakthrough could change the entire picture.

The most optimistic hope for substantial economy in computer composition depends on the perfection of an integrated, automatic system that performs all operations in one sequence. Because it now is possible to produce justified typesetting by computer, the next logical developments are machines that produce final page make-up automatically. This development would take full advantage of the speed inherent in automative processes.

The Linofilm composer and magnetic-tape system discussed briefly above are steps in the right direction but the need for an operator slows down the process. If the composer could be tape-controlled for automatic operation, an integrated system would be closer to reality. The simple items, such as folios that appear in a uniform position on all pages, would present no problems, but a complex layout on any page would make programming costs prohibitive. All these factors must be carefully weighed before choosing computer composition. This is a field to watch for it has tremendous potentials that are being developed.

12

SUMMARY OF THE MOST COMMON CATALOG DEFICIENCIES

In this chapter a negative approach is used to ensure that positive results are obtained from your catalog. Have you ever attempted to put on a potential client's hat and review your catalog from his point of view? This is the most critical review of a catalog. How well would your catalog survive this type of criticism? The answer to this question indicates catalog effectiveness. Monday-morning quarterbacking is a sport indulged in by many; it can be used to advantage by applying similar practices to your catalog review. Perform your Monday-morning quarterbacking, however, before the catalog is printed or distributed. This chapter discusses two of the most common faults present in catalog programs and concludes with a catalog checklist. Remember, you must be the catalog's severest critic. Do not give potential clients a catalog with which you are not completely satisfied.

WHITE-SPACE FACTOR

The white-space factor is taken into consideration during the page layout phase of the catalog program. It relates to the amount of material on a page versus the page size. An error often committed is to jam as much copy on a page as possible. Pages that are saturated with copy do not provide a pleasing presentation. The solid page usually is more difficult to read and offers no possible solution for including material that should be added in a later catalog edition.

There is a strong feeling among many catalog producers that they must fill every page solid to get their money's worth. There is no question that they do get more words and facts in the catalog in this way, but at what price? The catalog is more difficult to use and offers no chance for making later additions except by a completely new layout.

Maintaining the balance of white space on a page is a design function of the artist. Most artists have very good judgment on this subject but have very little say about it. This is unfortunate since presentation is such an important issue in a catalog. Check your catalog for this white-space factor. Does the material look cramped or is there a comfortable balance on each page? Glance through other catalogs and observe the white-space factor. In most cases you will find that catalogs with the most white space provide the most pleasing presentations.

Often it is not realized that the physical aspects of the catalog reflect the pride and attitude that a company has in its products. A well-designed catalog can be used as a public relations tool to help influence the minds of customers. An excellent product can be made to appear mediocre through poor catalog presentations; likewise, an average product can gain prestige through good catalog presentation. In other words the graphic elements of a catalog are important and should be handled with professionalism. The white-space factor rates as one of the more significant graphic elements. Use it to advantage. Do not present an overcrowded look to potential clients.

MULTIPLE-PURPOSE CATALOGS

Another common error in catalog programs is that many are designed for multiple purposes. Anything that detracts from the basic selling purpose of the catalog should be omitted. If the catalog is successful and is selling products, it is doing its job. Do not overburden it with other tasks. This cannot help but reduce its over-all effectiveness. If an installation procedure for a device is simple and is a selling point, it could be included. If installation instructions add nothing to the sales pitch, do not include them; package them in the delivery box, not in the catalog. Superfluous material adds only to the page count not to the usefulness of the catalog. Remember, catalog size has a direct bearing on the ease of use.

To determine whether material should be included, simply ask the question, "Will this help sell the product or service?" An affirmative answer justifies its presence, a negative answer should dictate its elimination from consideration. Review catalog material in this manner and see how many negative answers you find. If there are negative answers, do something about them before printing and distributing the catalog.

CATALOG CHECKLIST

There are several items that should be checked before releasing the catalog for printing. This is the final opportunity to see how you have anticipated your reader.

Cover

The cover is the first contact a client has with a catalog. Will the cover design make a favorable impression? Does it clearly portray the contents and identify the company? Is a number assigned to it so that the catalog can be referenced easily? Are you satisfied with the binding used? Will it perform properly and is it compatible with the size of the catalog? Is the cover material compatible with the cover design?

Index and Organization

These two factors are too closely related to separate. If the catalog is organized properly, the indexing should be a reasonably simple task. To verify the usability of the index try to find a specific item in the catalog. A better test is to have someone unfamiliar with the catalog try to find a particular product. Circulate preliminary copies of the catalog to your entire sales force. Get their opinions. After all, they probably will be using it more than anyone else. Is the index easy to understand and use? Does it clearly differentiate between major product lines? Is the catalog organization the best possible?

Front Matter Material

It is important to check that the treatment of front matter material is consistent with the body of the catalog. The front matter pages serve as the catalog introduction. Often the front matter is taken for granted. Do not make this mistake; no page in a sales catalog should be overlooked. The function of the catalog is too important to chance boring potential users. Great tasks have been completed to get the catalog in their hands, so make these tasks worthwhile by presenting the most interesting catalog possible. Is the front matter concise and to the point? Eliminate any long-winded dissertations that tend to creep into introductions and company history pages.

Catalog Body

The catalog body certainly must rate as the most important part of the catalog. The first check should be for product coverage. Is each product given full treatment? Anticipate questions that might be asked. The sales department should give valuable aid here; salesmen most likely are the recipients of most inquiries on your products. Next, the over-all presentation of each single or two-page spread should be evaluated. Check for fancy arrangements in basic page layouts. Remember, the eye is most accustomed to symmetrical patterns. It is irritating to make the user follow unusual patterns. Ease of comparison between text and illustration and family associations are important. Are the proper points emphasized? Are enough titles and subtitles used? Are two-page spreads properly linked together? Are there large areas of text that could be broken up for easier reading? Are all charts and graphs presented in their simplest form? Are all references correct? Is information given that leads the user to the next step toward making a sale?

Illustrations

Are all illustrations in their simplest form, do they clearly depict what was intended, and are they sized properly? In many cases illustrations are considered the most important part of the catalog. Preparing technical text is a matter of developing motivation. A good illustration helps considerably and many times is absolutely essential. In some markets, particularly the domestic market, the starting point of the catalog could well be the planning of illustrations. This includes setting the staging and hiring models and commercial photographers.

If illustrations are supplied to the printer separately from the reproducible text, they must be keyed carefully. Only by careful keying will the printer know exactly where each illustration is located. Also check all reduction instructions. Will the reduced illustration fit into the spot allocated to it in the page layout?

Use of Color

In the preprinting phase it is sometimes difficult to evaluate the use of additional colors in the catalog. This is best performed by artists with trained, critical eyes. Are you making maximum use of the color? There is a tendency to overwork colors so that the basic message is either lost or confused. Color is usually used for emphasis, indexing, or tying information together. Do not use color just for the sake of having a second color. When you use it, make it work for you. This will provide a better, more useful product. Wasted color often does more harm than good.

Catalog Design

Catalog design can include many evils. In the context of this discussion it means the over-all presentation, that provided by the blending of proper type selection with a tasteful standard format and good illustrations. There should be a pattern of consistency that is evident when thumbing page-by-page through the catalog. You should get a feeling that all pages belong and that they are linked in some manner. This can be accomplished by standard format, color, and presentation. No single page or two-page spread should be more outstanding than the others with the exception of the cover. There should be a harmonious impression created throughout the entire catalog.

Marketing Plan and Distribution

The occasion for distributing new catalogs affords a perfect opportunity to develop interest in your products. A promotion campaign, beginning with a predistribution piece to announce the new catalog, should be started. Another consideration at this time is the design of the envelope or carton that will be used to mail the catalog. It should clearly announce its contents. Is the advertising department aware of the shipping date of the catalogs? Are they, or you, doing anything about it? A considerable investment has been made to get the catalog program this far, by all means do not stop now. Promote the catalog with whatever funds remain in the catalog program.

Are you prepared for distributing your catalog? For large distributions, there is a tremendous logistics problem. A large crew of clerks must be ready when the catalogs are received to get them into the mail as fast as possible. Timing is an important factor in the highly competitive world of today; every day counts. Consult the printer for possible direct shipments from his plant. Many larger printing houses are equipped for large mailings. If not, it may be possible to coordinate your mailing with a direct-mail agency equipped with automatic machinery. Be prepared for distribution; this is a big job that is often underestimated.

SUMMARY

If your catalog has successfully passed the tests given in the checklist, it is ready to be released for printing, with distribution just a step away. You must feel confident that the catalog is exactly what you want. Once it hits the field it is too late. If you are confident, you will be rewarded by an effective catalog. If you have some doubts, make amendments even at this late date. There is no doubt that a new catalog has sales impact when it is distributed. The rewards of months of planning and hard work should soon be evident.

INDEX